Patchwork Quilts
to make for children

Patchwork Quilts
to make for children

MARGARET ROLFE

British Library Cataloguing in Publication Data
Rolfe, Margaret
    Patchwork quilts to make for children.
    1. Patchwork quilts. Making. Manuals
    746.46

    ISBN 0-7153-9777-X

First published in Great Britain
by David & Charles 1989

First published in Australia in 1989
by Greenhouse Publications Pty Ltd
122-126 Ormond Road
Elwood Victoria 3184 Australia

Printed in Singapore
for David & Charles Publishing plc
Brunel House   Newton Abbot   Devon

Distributed in the U.S.A. by
Sterling Publishing Co. Inc.
387 Park Avenue South
New York, N.Y. 10016

Contents

A word from the author
Acknowledgements   vi

I Techniques and Construction   1

Equipment   2

Materials   4

Piecing   6

Applique   18

Embroidery stitches   22

Quilting   23

Quilt and cushion construction   27

II Patterns and Projects

Simple Squares   32
  Tied bassinet quilt   32
  Machine quilted cot quilt   33

Talking point quilt   34

Teddy Bear Log Cabin quilt   36

Football stripes quilt and cushions   38

Doll's quilts   41
  Pinwheel quilt   41
  Triangle mosaic quilt   42
  Basket quilt   43
  Dresden plate quilt   44

Train quilt   45

Farm Life quilt   47

Alphabet quilt   59

Dinosaur continental quilt cover   72

Elephant quilt   78

Sheep on Clover quilt   80

Scotty dog quilt   82

Zoo quilt   84

Benjamin Bunny and Friends quilt   98

Bunnyrun quilt   100

Panda quilt   102

Penguin Parade quilt   104

Polar bear wall hanging   106

Puffin bag   109

Ladybird bag   111

Toucan backpack   112

Ele's Embroidered quilt   114

Miss Mouse quilt   118

Advent Calendar quilt   132

Teddy Bear, Teddy Bear quilt   139

Glossary of quilting terms   150

Index   151

A word from the author . . .

The first quilt that I ever made was an alphabet cot quilt for my daughter who arrived not long before I discovered the joys of quiltmaking. Now that baby daughter is a teenager. In the intervening time, I have learnt and taught quiltmaking skills, and I have learnt to create patchwork designs. While this book offers some tried and true traditional patterns, it also offers new and original pieced block designs, using the 'straight line patchwork' system which I have developed. Traditional patchwork patterns rely primarily on combinations of squares, rectangles and right angle triangles. With my designs, it is possible to sew any geometric shape, yet still sew the pieces together in easy-to-seam straight lines. I present these designs in quilts for you to make, but I hope that they will encourage you to think of lots of new ideas and many ways to use them.

Our children are the adults of tomorrow, and there should be no task more worthwhile than raising these future citizens. Women generally have carried this burden devotedly and often through unrecognised and unsung labour. I firmly believe that time spent with our children should be valued for its fundamental importance and that time is well spent that lovingly introduces them to this world made richer by Beatrix Potter and Claude Monet.

I hope that people will use my patterns and designs to create quilts that children will love. I remember how my own children loved the soft toys I sewed for them more than many shop bought ones. If this book succeeds in the way that is important to me, its memorial will be found in ragged and tatty remnants of very well loved quilts.

Acknowledgements

A book like this would not come into being were it not for the work of a whole team of people. First, I must give tribute to the creativity and skill of my friends who made such superb quilts for the book. I am indebted to Margaret Barclay, Trudy Brodie, Kerry Gavin, Ann Haddad, Edna Hayden, Beryl Hodges, Linda McGuire, Beth Miller, Vivienne Mildren, Elizabeth Russo, Christa Roksandic, Beverley Sach, Wendy Saclier, Pam Taylor, and Judy Turner for all their magnificent work. Special thanks to Judy Turner for also generously sharing her wealth of technical knowledge about quiltmaking.

Other people help in a multitude of ways; by lending books, making design suggestions and criticism, finding and lending photographic props, and generally by giving moral and physical support to the whole project. I am grateful to them all. I would like to specially thank Joan Fitzgerald, my extra pair of hands; Mary Greeshaw, my good neighbour; my children Phil and Mindy, for their contributions to the designs; my son Bernie, for solving computer problems; my parents Linda and Alex Poppins, for helping in every way possible; my brother Patrick Poppins and sister-in-law Colleen Moore, for allowing us to invade their house for photography; Kay Le Lievre, for making the doorstop mouse; Monica and Lachlan Poppins, my niece and nephew, for being such delightful models; Mike Fisher, for his excellent photography; and most of all my husband Barry, for his unfailing support and encouragement.

Margaret Rolfe, 1989

I

Techniques and construction

Equipment

Measurement

All dimensions are given in both the metric and imperial measurements, the latter being marked by square brackets, e.g. [1″]. Note that the two systems *are not interchangeable* as only whole figure equivalents have been used. Use only one system in any one project, as the measurements for each project have been worked out independently for both systems to enable simple multiples to be used. For example 12 inches may be equivalents of either 32 cm or 30 cm, depending on whether it is divided by a multiple of 3 or 4.

Templates, block and border sizes are all given *without seam allowances added*. The only exception to this are the measurements given for cutting binding strips which have all been worked out to include seam allowances in them. All other measurements need to have seams added.

Sewing machine

Your machine is the most important piece of equipment for quiltmaking. It does not have to do fancy stitches; just straight stitching and a zigzag that will give a smooth satin stitch is sufficient.

Quilting hoop

A hoop is used to hold the three layers of the quilt sandwich in place as you stitch them together in the quilting process. The hoop stops the layers from shifting as you quilt, and also supports the work leaving your hands free to stitch. The hoop consists of two wooden rings, one of which fits inside the other. The inner hoop is laid down, the quilt put smoothly across it, then the outer hoop is pressed down on top. A hoop about 35–40 cm (14″–16″) in diameter is a good size, although larger hoops can be used. The length of your arm will determine which size of hoop is most comfortable. If you have longer arms, you may prefer a larger hoop.

Scissors

Sharp dressmaking scissors are essential for cutting fabrics. Use a different pair of scissors for cutting out paper and cardboard. A small pair of pointed sharp scissors are needed for embroidery and applique.

Needles

For hand piecing and applique, select the size of needle that is comfortable for you to use. For embroidery, select a crewel needle with an eye large enough to fit the embroidery thread. For quilting, either a size 8 or 9 between needle should be suitable.

Pins

Pins are required at all stages for patchwork. For most patchwork and quilting berry pins are the handiest to use (and they are easy to see when accidentally dropped). However, for machine applique, you will need regular dressmaking pins.

Thimble

Quilting is much more comfortable if a thimble is worn. If you are not used to wearing a thimble, persist in trying one just for quilting, because the thimble protects your fingers as you push the needle through the layers of a quilt. Choose a thimble that fits your finger without being uncomfortably tight or so loose that it falls off. Some people like to use two thimbles when they quilt: one on the traditional third finger of the sewing hand to push the needle; and a second on the pointer finger of the other hand to protect the finger which guides the needle back up through the quilt. Alternatively, instead of a second thimble, the pointer finger can be protected by a leather thimble or piece of sticking plaster.

Iron

As the patchwork pieces are stitched together, each seam needs to be pressed carefully so that the next piece to be sewn will fit accurately. Do not iron too vigorously, or the patchwork will become stretched and distorted; just press gently. Steam pressing will assist making the pieces lie flat, particularly at bulky seam joins. Always press the finished patchwork well before putting the layers together ready for quilting as once the batting is added, you cannot iron it again without flattening the batting completely. A spray container filled with water is useful for dampening difficult bits ready for pressing.

Square of paper

A sheet of paper approximately 40 cm [16"] square is needed to lay out the pieces of your patchwork block after you have cut them out. The pieces can be pinned to the paper so they stay in place until you are ready to sew. Laying the pieces out also helps you put them together the correct way round.

Sandpaper

A sheet of fine sandpaper is very useful to position underneath the fabric when marking around a template. The sandpaper prevents the fabric from slipping under the template, particularly when you are marking small pieces. Glue the sandpaper to a piece of thin chipboard to make it more solid and durable.

Rulers

An ordinary ruler is necessary for drawing the designs on to graph paper when making templates. Two special rulers are made just for quiltmaking. A small narrow ruler (sometimes called a 'quilters quarter') is the width of a seam allowance to help you mark them accurately. The second type is a long transparent ruler with markings both lengthwise and crosswise to be used in conjunction with a rotary cutter.

Set square

A large clear plastic set square with a 45° angle is needed to make accurate angles. It is also used in conjunction with a rotary cutter. A set square about 18 cm [7"] along each side of the right angle is a convenient size.

Rotary cutter and mat

A rotary cutter is a very sharp circular blade on a handle, used to cut strips and other regular shaped patches. It is a modern invention that makes fast and efficient work of the time consuming chore of marking and cutting out each patch. A special mat is needed underneath the fabric as you cut. The largest size mat is most useful.

Pencils

Sharp HB pencils are required to draw the design and mark most fabrics. Use a white or yellow coloured pencil to mark dark coloured fabrics. You will also need a small set of coloured pencils to colour in the templates of the pictorial block designs. This helps you match the correct template with a particular piece of fabric. A good pencil sharpener is necessary as your pencils must be well sharpened to ensure accurate marking.

Glue stick

When making templates use a glue stick to paste your drawn design onto cardboard.

Sticky tape and masking tape

Sticky tape is used to hold templates in place when you are using a rotary cutter. Masking tape can be useful as a guide for quilting lines.

Materials

Fabrics

The most suitable fabrics for patchwork are cotton and cotton polyester mix fabrics which have a firm and even weave. You can use poplin, polypoplin, calico, homespun, lawn, in fact, most dress-weight fabrics. Other fabrics can be used, but they may be more difficult to sew. Thicker fabrics will create more bulky seam allowances, and will be more difficult to quilt. If you are in doubt about your choice of fabric try out a small sample first. Thinner fabrics such as lawn can be very useful to back quilts as they are soft and easy to hand quilt.

> *Prewash and iron all the fabrics before you use them, to safeguard against colour running and shrinkage.*
>
> The quantities of fabric listed for quilts in this book are all based on fabric which is 114 cm [45"] wide. An extra 25% needs to be added for fabrics which are 90 cm [36"] wide.

Padding

Polyester batting is the most widely available and practical material for the padding layer in quilting. It comes in a variety of thicknesses, so choose a thickness suitable for your project. Clothing may require a very thin batting, whilst quilts need a thicker batting. Very thick batting is not a good choice because it is very difficult to quilt, although it can be used for a tied quilt. Use thin firm batting for all strip quilting. Cotton and cotton and polyester mix batting is obtainable, and can be used, although the pure cotton will require close quilting so that it does not bunch up with washing and wearing.

Threads

Thread for piecing. For both hand piecing and machine piecing, use a good quality machine sewing thread. If you are machine piecing, white thread can generally be used throughout. If you are hand piecing, match the thread to the darker of the two fabrics being sewn together.

Thread for hand applique. Use good quality dressmaking threads in colours to match the applique pieces.

Thread for machine applique. While ordinary dressmaking threads can be used, machine embroidery thread is preferable.

Thread for embroidery. Stranded embroidery cotton is suggested for the embroidery in this book. You can make the thread thicker or thinner by changing the number of strands you use. Stranded embroidery thread comes in a wide variety of colours.

Thread for hand quilting. Quilting requires a strong thread which will not break easily with the constant rubbing through the eye of the needle. For hand quilting, use the quilting thread made especially for this purpose. White or cream quilting thread is used for a traditional effect, and because the hand quilting stitch creates a broken line, you will find that white or cream will blend in to most colours. However, today there is a variety of coloured quilting threads available so you can match the quilting thread to the colour of the fabric. There are no rights and wrongs about this; choose either white or coloured thread to give the effect you want.

Thread for machine quilting. For machine quilting, use a good quality machine sewing thread. Match the top thread to the colour of your patchwork, choosing either a specific colour to match a fabric in the quilt, or a colour that will match the overall tone of colour in the quilt. Match the bobbin thread to the colour of the backing fabric. Clear polyester thread is an alternative top thread, as it will blend into all colours. Use the polyester thread on the top only, and use ordinary thread on the bobbin, to prevent snarls occurring.

Graph paper

Large sheets of graph paper (A3 or A2 size) are needed on which to draw templates. Graph paper makes drawing templates easy as right angles are all correct, and measurements can be made from the grid.

Cardboard

Large sheets of cardboard will be needed to make templates. Eight sheet pasteboard is an ideal weight. Plastic template material made especially for quilting can be used in place of cardboard if preferred. For some applique you will need a light weight cardboard (about the weight of the paper in greeting cards).

Piecing

Most women today are fortunate to have a choice between hand or machine piecing. Their lifestyle will probably determine the choice. Some like to machine piece because it is quick and strong, while others like to hand piece because it is a relaxing activity and a break from the demands of the rest of their lives. Either way is correct; you should choose what is right for you and your needs.

> There are, however, differences in approaching the sewing, notably in making templates and marking the fabrics, so your decision to either hand or machine sew will affect the way you proceed from the very beginning.

Hand piecing

For all hand piecing, make templates without a seam allowance. In other words, the template shape is the shape of the patch after it has been sewn. When you mark the fabric around the template the line you draw is your *stitching line*.

Making templates for hand piecing

• Using graph paper, for both convenience and accuracy, draw your patchwork shape.

• Paste the graph paper to cardboard. Do not cut out the shape first because you get a more accurate result if you cut out both graph paper and cardboard in one operation.

• Cut out the template shape.

• Label with size, and mark grain line, marking both front and back (the reverse) of template if necessary (see page 11).

Marking and cutting the fabric

• Place fabric (prewashed and pressed), wrong side facing up, on top of your sandpaper board.

• Place template shape on top of fabric, matching the grain line on the template with the grain of the fabric.

• Using a *sharp* pencil, mark around template. Leave 2 cm [¾"] between any two shapes, for the seam allowances.

• Cut out the shapes, leaving a 6 mm [¼"] seam allowance all around.

Stitching and pressing

• Match the colour of the thread you use to the darker of the fabrics which you are piecing together. An ordinary dressmaking thread is satisfactory.

• Pin pieces together matching corners exactly.

• Sew along the marked lines using a running stitch, with an occasional back stitch to add strength. Begin with a knot and a back stitch, and end with several back stitches. Sew only along the marked line, and not over the seam allowances which should be allowed to sit freely.

• After the block is sewn, press all seams to one side (see page 12).

Machine piecing

There are two methods of machine-piecing and you should choose the method according to the shapes that you are using and the method you feel most comfortable with.

Piecing with marked seam allowances

This method involves making templates that are *the exact size of your patch*, drawing this shape onto the fabric and then machine stitching along the marked pencil lines. *When you mark, the pencil line becomes your stitching line*, and you cut out each patch allowing a seam allowance all around which you judge by eye. It is almost the same approach as is used for hand piecing, the only difference is that with machine piecing you generally sew across the seam allowances.

Piecing with marked seam allowances can be done for all shapes, whether they are regular symmetrical shapes or irregular asymmetrical shapes. *This method is the only satisfactory one to use when making the pictorial blocks that are a feature of this book.* Some people like to do all their piecing by this method because it is very precise and accurate. Its disadvantage is that each piece must be marked before stitching, and you cannot use the quick rotary cutter methods for cutting out.

Piecing with automatic seam allowances

This approach works for all regular shapes, such as squares, rectangles, and triangles which are divisions of a square; the shapes which are the basis of most traditional patchwork patterns. Exact seam allowances are included in each patch you cut out, and the pieces are sewn together by lining up the cut edges. Templates are made that have an exact seam allowance added (templates with automatic seam allowances). *When you mark, the pencil line becomes your cutting line*. Your sewing line is judged by lining up the foot of your machine with the cut edge so that you stitch exactly the seam allowance required. Piecing with automatic seam allowances works with regular shapes because when you cut out two of these shapes and place them one on top of each other, they fit exactly, with no guessing as to where the seams should be. Irregular asymmetrical shapes do not fit together like this, and so it is very much more difficult to match up the corners properly.

Two regular symmetrical shapes will match exactly when they are placed right sides together.

Two irregular shapes will not match exactly when they are placed right sides together.

Piecing with automatic seam allowances is time saving because you do not need to pin patches together, at least at the beginning when you first join the patches together. Pins are only needed later when you need to match seam junctions. Another time saver is that the rotary cutter can be used to cut the patches, and this removes the necessity for any marking at all. Also the rotary cutter can cut through several layers at once, so a speedy job can be made of cutting out.

> I suggest you use both approaches to piecing, depending on the shapes in the project you are making. The pictorial blocks must be pieced by using marked seam lines, but any of the patchwork with simple regular shapes can be pieced with automatic seam allowances.

Both approaches can be used for different parts of a quilt, for instance with the Zoo quilt (page 84) the alternate patchwork blocks can be pieced with automatic seam allowances, while the pictorial animal blocks should be pieced by following marked seam lines. Just keep in mind the fundamental difference between the two approaches.

You may be one of the people who is more comfortable with doing all your machine piecing with marked seam lines. If so, just follow the procedures for machine piecing pictorial blocks for both kinds of shapes.

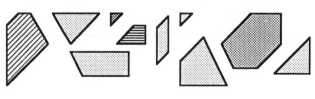

Pictorial blocks and machine piecing

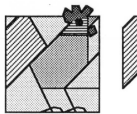 

A feature of this book is the new and original set of pictorial block designs. These pictorial blocks have all been specially designed so that they can be machine pieced with all straight line sewing. The concept behind this *straight line piecing* is quite simple. It rests on the idea that when shapes are joined together, the order in which they are pieced can determine whether the seams are simple straight lines, or not so simple seams with awkward corners. Of course it is possible to sew awkward corners, but it is fiddly and difficult. Another advantage of the system is that any irregular geometric shape can be included in a design, so that the designs move beyond the squares, rectangles and right angle triangles of traditional patchwork.

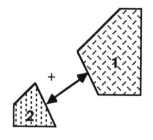 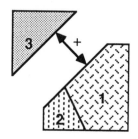

By showing the seams by a + sign, the piecing order can be described in steps:

    1   1 + 2

The pieces already joined are shown in brackets (1−2).

The second step is to join piece 3, shown thus:

    2   (1−2) + 3

Piecing order

Straight line piecing

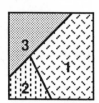 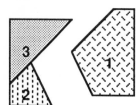

The pictorial blocks have all been carefully designed so that every seam will be a straight line, and there will be no awkward corners *if you follow the piecing order given*. To help you with this, the designs are presented in a novel way. Each piece in the design is numbered, and then the piecing order involves following a step-by-step sequence. The seams are represented by a + (an adding) sign.

Patchwork block with pieces numbered.

If pieces 2 and 3 are stitched first, piece 1 is awkward to add.

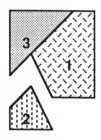 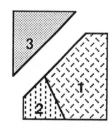

Piece 2 is awkward if 1 and 2 are joined first.

If 1 and 2 are joined first, adding piece 3 is an easy straight seam.

Sewing pieces one and two together is shown thus:

    1 + 2

Once joined together, the pieces are represented by numbers in brackets, thus the pieces one and two joined together are shown:

    (1−2)

If piece three is to be joined to the unit of one and two, it is indicated by:

    (1−2) + 3

This then creates a new unit, described as:

(**1–3**)

The steps in the piecing order sequence would look like this this:

1 **1 + 2**
2 (**1–2**) + **3**

Sometimes the units or pieces will be left aside, and will be joined in later. So the next step could be:

3 **4 + 5 + 6**

Then the two units can be joined together to make a new unit:

4 (**1–3**) + (**4–6**)

Designs which might appear to be complex, become quite simple by this method. Once you understand how the system works, you will become adept at working out the piecing order yourself.

> It is a good idea to keep the diagram of the block and piecing order next to you as you sew, especially when you are new to it. Try one of the easiest blocks to begin with; one with only a few pieces such as the rooster (see page 56) or the cat (see page 58).

Piecing order

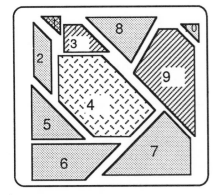

Block laid out ready to sew. Pin pieces in their correct places to a sheet of paper.

1. **1 + 2**

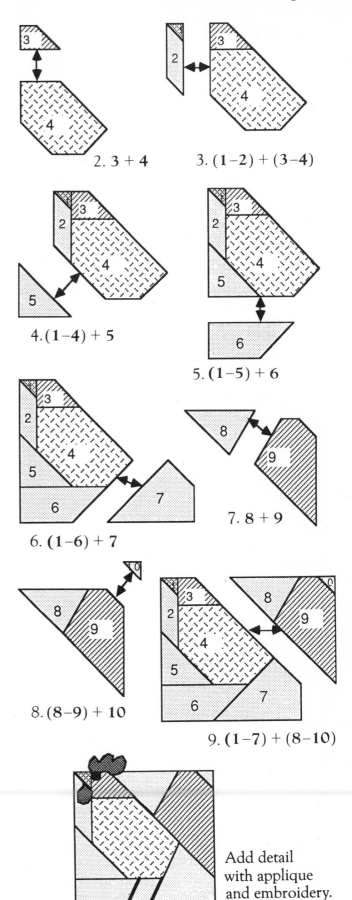

2. **3 + 4**

3. (**1–2**) + (**3–4**)

4. (**1–4**) + **5**

5. (**1–5**) + **6**

6. (**1–6**) + **7**

7. **8 + 9**

8. (**8–9**) + **10**

9. (**1–7**) + (**8–10**)

Add detail with applique and embroidery.

Working with the grids

The block designs are all presented on grids. For instance, many of the designs are based on a grid of 8 x 8 squares, where each square can represent 3 cm [1¼″] to make a 24 cm [10″] block size. Your first step is to enlarge the design to the size you want by drawing it on to graph paper.

Using grids has one great advantage. Because you draw the entire block, full size, to make the templates, and then cut it out, you can be totally confident that your templates are accurate because what you cut apart must fit back together again exactly. So it does not even matter if your design is slightly different when you draw it (you may even want to deliberately make some changes). Because you began with the full block, your templates must be accurate. It is just like a jigsaw puzzle. Drawing the designs on to a grid also means that you can easily change the size of the designs by changing the size of the grid.

Tips to help you make pictorial blocks

• It is important to *number the templates*, so you know where they fit in the design once it is cut up. Colouring them also helps. When you mark the fabric it is a good idea to mark the number of each piece unobtrusively in the seam allowance; just in case later you wonder which piece is which.

• *Notches* have been marked on some pieces of the designs, usually on triangular shaped pieces. It is very easy to turn a triangle around when you pick it up, and then be unsure which side you are meant to be sewing. A notch marked on one side of the triangle and on the side of the piece to which it will be joined will be a help. Mark notches on the seam allowances with pencil.

• Note that most of the designs are asymmetrical (which means there is nowhere you can divide them down the middle and find two halves the same). *If you want to have the design face the same way as shown, you will need to mark the wrong side of the fabric with your templates face down. To have the design face the opposite way, you will need to mark with the templates face up.*

• Some of the designs occasionally include some very small pieces. The secret of coping with these is to make extra large seam allowances. *When you are marking and cutting out small small pieces, allow a full 2 cm (¾″) seam allowance.* The extra fabric can

easily be trimmed away after the seam has been sewn, but the larger allowance makes small pieces much easier to pin and sew together.

• *Before you start sewing, it is very important to lay out the block, with all the pieces in their correct places.* I suggest pinning all the pieces to a square of paper. After sewing each seam make sure that you put the pieces back in their correct place. It is also a good idea to lay out the block for traditional patchwork blocks. They are then safe from the depredations of wind, children and pets!

Making templates for a pictorial block

• Using a coloured pencil draw the grid onto graph paper. For example, one square might equal 3 cm [1¼″].

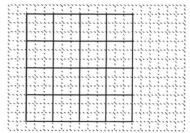

• Draw the block design onto the grid and number all the pieces. Remember that it will not matter if the design is not exactly the same as that given; the templates will be accurate anyway. Mark any notches.

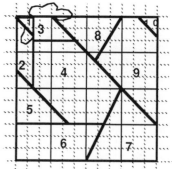

• Colour in the pieces of the design. (This can be a rough job; just enough to indicate the colour of each piece.) Using your glue stick, *paste the whole block to the cardboard and then cut.* This gives the most accurate result.

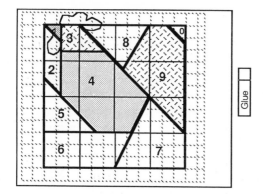

• Cut out the template pieces.

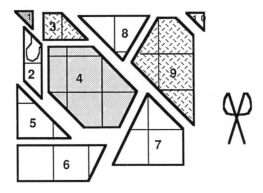

• Mark the grain line and notches on both sides of the template. On the grid side, just mark a line along any one of the grid lines. If the template shape has one or more edges parallel to the grain line, you can easily mark the grain on both the top and back (reverse) of the template by just drawing a line parallel to this edge.

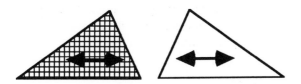

If none of the edges of the template are parallel to the grain line, mark the grain line on the reverse side by using a pin to pierce through the cardboard template at two points along any of the lines on the graph paper. Turn the template over and draw a line between the two pin holes.

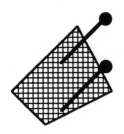

Marking and cutting the fabric, and laying out the block

• Place prewashed and pressed fabric wrong side up on top of your sandpaper board.

• Match the grain line on the template with the grain of the fabric, except on special occasions when you might want to take advantage of a particular pattern or motif on the fabric.

Using a sharp pencil draw around the template. (Use a white or yellow pencil on dark fabrics.) Leave enough fabric around each piece to make a 6 mm [¼"] seam. For small pieces, leave wider seam allowances approximately 2 cm [¾"] *Note that the line you draw is your sewing line, not your cutting line.*

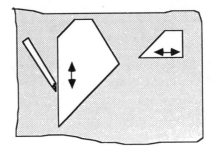

• Mark the number of each piece on the seam allowance.

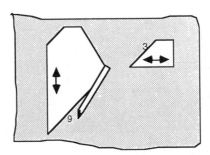

• Cut out the pieces with the seam allowances.

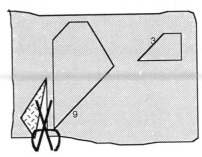

• Lay out the block onto a square of paper. Pin the pieces to the paper.

Pinning pieces together

If you are machine piecing following marked seam allowances, it is essential that you pin carefully and accurately. *The corners must meet exactly.* The process is easy if you follow these four simple steps:

• With right sides of the patches together, poke pins through at the marked corners of each patch. Do not try at this stage to push the pins back up through the fabrics.

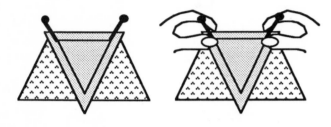

• Using both hands, hold the patch at each corner, then gently pull along the seam line. This should align the two seam lines along the length of the two patches.

• Pin along the length of the marked line, checking both sides to see that the pins are accurately on the line. Place the pins so that the pointed ends are towards the end from which you will start sewing.

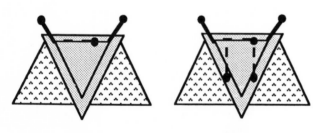

• Place several extra pins at right angles to the seam line, including a pin each end. Place the pins so that they are a little distance way from the sewing line and will not get in the way of the presser foot.

Stitching

Stitch the pinned pieces together, keeping exactly on the marked line. Pull out the pins down the seam line just before you come to them. Stitch from cut edge to cut edge, across the seam allowances but you do not need to back track. Trim the thread ends away. If you make a habit of always doing this immediately after each seam, your work will not only look much neater, but the ends will not get in the way of later sewing. Where there are wide seam allowances for small pieces, trim these back after the seam is stitched.

Remember to follow the piecing order given so that all seams are straight seams.

Pressing

Press seams immediately after each seam is sewn. It is very important to have seams pressed before you stitch across them, otherwise the block will not sit flat, and subsequent seams will not be accurate. The seams should be pressed to one side. There are several factors which will determine which direction to press the seam allowances:

• Press seam allowances away from where any quilting will go. It is always easier to quilt through an area that has only a single layer of fabric above the batting.

• Press seam allowances towards the side of the darker fabric, so that they do not create a shadow under a light fabric.

• Press seam allowances in the direction which will help the block to sit flat. In other words, try not to force bulky seam allowances in directions they do not naturally wish to lie.

• Press the seam allowances in opposite directions at a seam junction.

Occasionally, when there is a big junction of many seams, it helps the block to sit flat by pressing the seam allowances open. (This is sometimes suggested in the instructions.)

Machine piecing regular shapes

Squares, rectangles and some right angle triangles (those which are divisions of a square) are regular symmetrical shapes, and are the easiest to piece (sew together). These shapes are the basis of most traditional patchwork patterns.

As with all patchwork, accuracy is important. A small error may seem inconsequential on one piece but when that same error is repeated many times, the work will become quite distorted. For instance, cutting one patch just 3 mm [⅛″] short may seem trivial, but when that is repeated 8 times, an error of over 2 cm [1″] occurs.

While regular shapes can be sewn together following the method for irregular shapes and hand piecing, you will find it easier and quicker to cut out your patches of fabric with an exact seam allowance all around; that is with an automatic seam allowance. You do not need to mark a stitching line, because you can just put the patches one on top of each other and sew them together using a 6 mm [¼″] seam. Because the shapes are regular and symmetrical, when you put the patches one on top of each other they will match exactly, and they should not even need to be pinned together. However, pins will be needed when you want to match seams junctions.

There are two basic ways of cutting your fabric patches with automatic seam allowances.

The first way is to mark the fabric from templates which already have a seam allowance included then cut out the marked shapes with scissors.

The second method is to use a rotary cutter. It makes quick work of cutting as it is possible to stack fabrics so that several patches are cut out at once. The time spent in cutting out a quilt can be halved or even quartered and the chore of marking is eliminated.

There are some situations where it is not appropriate to use the rotary cutter. When you want to select part of the pattern on the fabric, such as a stripe as or a special motif, or if the pattern is one directional, it is better to cut out the shapes individually with scissors.

Making templates with seam allowance added

Templates made this way are also called templates with automatic seam allowances.

• Using graph paper to give accuracy (both for measurement and angles), draw the exact shape you require. For example, if you need a 8 cm [3″] triangle, this is the shape you draw.

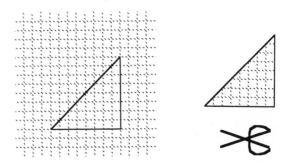

• Cut the graph paper shape out accurately.
• Paste the shape onto firm cardboard (or tape to template plastic), leaving a margin all around the shape.

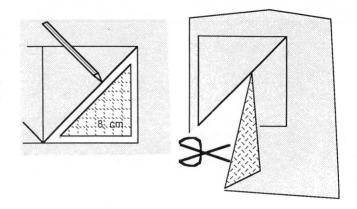

• Measure and draw a line exactly 6 mm [¼"] all around the shape. This can be done by using the special little patchwork ruler, the 'quilters quarter'. You can use an ordinary ruler but be sure to measure always at right angles to the edge of the shape.

• Cut out the cardboard shape. Label the template for future reference—e.g. 8 cm [3"] triangle, seams allowed, and mark the grain line.

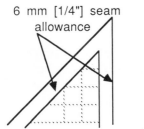

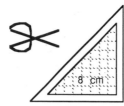

Marking and cutting the fabric with scissors

• Before you begin to mark the fabric, work out how best to arrange the pieces so that the best use can be made of the length of fabric. For instance, if there are long borders to be cut from the length of fabric, these are best cut first.

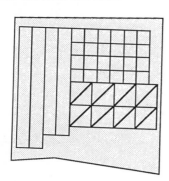

• Mark the fabric. Place your fabric on top of your sandpaper board so that it does not move while you are marking around the template. Using a sharp pencil, mark around the template. Keep your pencil well sharpened, and also keep the tip of the pencil as close to the template as possible so that no extra is added to the marking. As the seam allowance is included in the template, the shapes can be butted up to each other.

• Cut out the shapes following the pencil lines using sharp dressmaking scissors.

Cutting the fabric with a rotary cutter

To use this method, you will need a rotary cutter, a large cutting mat, a large clear plastic set square with a 45°, and a wide clear plastic patchwork ruler.

If you are working in imperial measurements (i.e. inches), templates often do not need to be made because the rulers are marked with imperial measurements, and these measurements can be used to cut the shapes you need.

When using metric measurements, or if you want to make triangles in either measurement system, or if you are making squares and rectangles bigger than your ruler allows, you can use a rotary cutter along with templates which have seam allowances added. Place the templates under the clear plastic ruler or set square, then use your rotary cutter to cut out the shapes.

It is a good idea to practise with the rotary cutter on some scrap fabric if you are not familiar with its use. The cutter needs to be very sharp, so replace the blades as soon as they become at all dull. Adjust the screw holding the blade in place so that the cutter works smoothly. Hold the cutter in your dominant hand (i.e. the right hand for right handed people, left hand for left handed people). The bulk of the fabric should be on the same side as your dominant hand and the edge to be cut and the ruler on the other side. The following instructions describe the procedure for a right handed person. Please make the necessary reversals to suit left handedness.

Practise holding the ruler firmly in one hand, while you run the cutter away from you along the edge of the ruler with the other hand. You will soon learn the amount of pressure you need to exert to make a clean cut. You may need to walk your fingers along the ruler as you cut, to keep the ruler from sliding. It is easier to work with a rotary cutter if you stand up over your cutting mat.

Squaring up the fabric

Before you begin to cut any shapes, it is very important to first square up the fabric.

• Fold fabric in half, selvedge edge next to selvedge edge, on top of your cutting mat. The selvedge edges should run left to right on the side furthest away from you, and the fold should run along the side nearest to you.

• Place a set square on the edge of the fold, making a right angle to the fold. Line the ruler up with the set square to make a right angle across the width of the material.

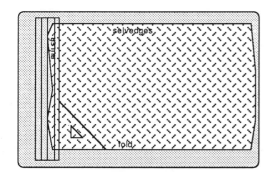

• Cut the fabric with the rotary cutter.

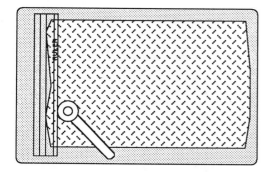

• Open out the fabric to check that the edge is straight like (a) and not a V-shape like (b) or (c).

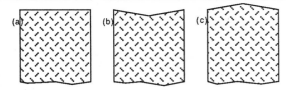

To make strips

• Fold the fabric either in half or in four, with the edge you have straightened on the left.

• Place the ruler on top of the fabric, and cut the strips, using the ruler alone or the ruler with template as a guide for the width.

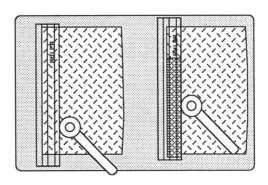

If you are using metric measurements, make a template the width of the strips, with 1.2 cm added for the seam allowances each side.

Place the template beneath the transparent ruler and use this as your guide (it can be held in place with sticky tape). The template itself should not be used because it could be accidentally cut, and so made unusable.

If you are working in imperial measurements, you can use the markings on the ruler as a guide to cut fabric into strips the required width. Note that this width will be the size of the strips *plus ½″ for the seam allowances.* For instance, if you need 2″ strips in the finished patchwork, cut the strips 2½″ wide.

To make squares and rectangles

• Cut the fabric into strips as described above.

• Next place the strips horizontally on the mat, and square up the end to be cut (which should be on the left side) using your set square. The fabric strips can be folded so that two or even four shapes are cut out at once.

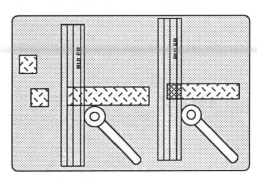

• Cut the strips into squares and rectangles, using the ruler or ruler and template as a guide.

To make triangles

Note that this system only works for right angle triangles which have 45° angles at the other two corners, i.e. they are triangles which are created by either dividing a square by cutting across either or both diagonals. The major difference between these two types of triangles in patchwork is how they relate to the straight grain of the fabric. With the one which is a division of a square into two, the straight grain will be on either of the shorter sides. With the triangle that is a division of a square into four, the straight grain goes on the hypotenuse, the longest side of the triangle.

• Fold the fabric either in half or in four, with the edge you have straightened on the left.

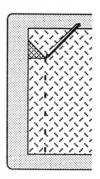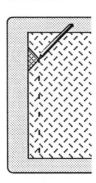

• Place your triangle template with the side which is to be on the grain exactly along the cut edge. With a sharp pencil, mark the fabric at the tip of the triangle farthest from the edge of the fabric. Repeat this several times so that you have several marks up and down the fabric.

• Align the edge of your clear plastic ruler with the pencil marks, and cut the strip.

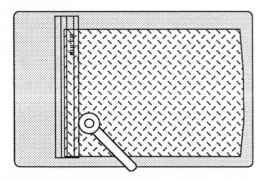

• Sticky tape your triangle template underneath your set square, placing the template so that its

edges exactly match the edges of one corner of your set square.

• Place one of the folded strips running left to right in front of you, and square up the left hand end with your set square if necessary. Using the template and set square as your guide, cut triangles along the length of the strip.

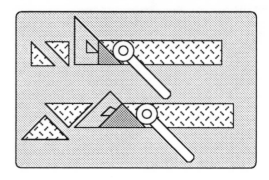

Sewing the pieces together

Piecing order

It is important to work out the piecing order before you begin to stitch the shapes together, so that you sew all straight seams. Generally small pieces of the block are sewn together first, then the pieces are sewn into rows, and finally the rows are put together to make a block.

Piecing order for regular shapes.

Piece small patches into units.

Piece units into rows.

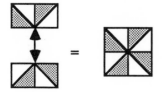

Piece rows into the block.

The log cabin block has its own order of piecing, beginning with the centre square. The strips are then sewn around this centre square, or, in the case of the courthouse steps variation, they are sewn either side of the centre square.

Piecing a log cabin block

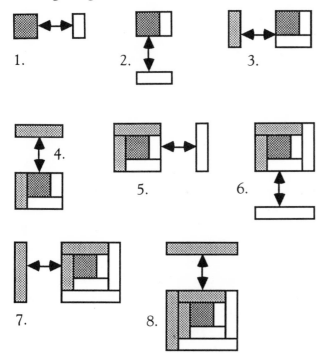

1. 2. 3.

4. 5. 6.

7. 8.

Piecing a log cabin block, courthouse steps variation.

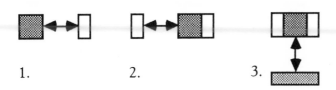

1. 2. 3.

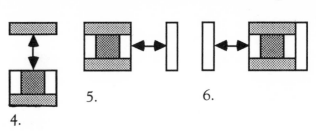

4.

5. 6.

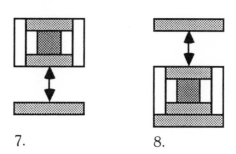

7. 8.

Sewing

Piecing with automatic seam allowances only works properly if you sew the same exact seam allowance that you have allowed for in your cutting. There are two methods of achieving this: first by learning to sew the 6 mm [¼″] by judging the distance with your eye (which can be done with practice), or, secondly, by adjusting your needle sideways (through the stitch width knob on your sewing machine) so that the edge of your foot is exactly 6 mm [¼″] from the needle. Keep a small scrap of graph paper near your machine so that you can set this distance accurately. Once the needle is adjusted, you can then use the edge of the foot as your guide, and just align the cut edges of the fabric with the edge of the foot.

• Sew shapes together. Lay shapes to be sewn exactly on top of each other, and stitch together using a 6 mm [¼″] seam. Stitch from cut edge to cut edge. Pinning should not be necessary. If there are lots of the same shapes to be joined, they can be fed through the machine in chain fashion.

• Press seams to one side (see page 12).

• Sew units together to make the block. Pinning will be necessary to make seam junctions accurate.

Applique

Hand applique

There are many different methods of approaching applique, but the following I have found to be the most useful.

• Prepare the background fabric. If you are going to applique a block design, cut a cardboard template the shape of your block. Draw around the template onto the wrong side of the background fabric. Draw a 6 mm [¼"] seam allowance all around the block, and cut out the block on this outside line. To save time, you may like to make your block template with the seam allowances already included. However, a drawn seam line is useful for indicating the edges of your design space, especially for designs which go close to the edge.

• Trace the applique design onto tracing paper. Mark grain lines vertically across the design so that each applique piece has a grain line going through it.

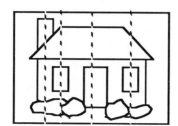

• Study the design and work out which pieces will overlap or underlap others. Mark the parts of pieces which will underlap by drawing a zigzag line, making the zigzag just inside the outline of the piece.

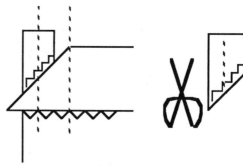

• Cut out each applique piece from the tracing paper. Don't cut out fiddly bits such as eyes, or other decorative details, because they can be added later, and will need separate patterns; just cut out all the major pieces. These now become your applique pattern pieces.

• Use the tracing paper patterns to cut out fabric shapes. Pin the tracing paper shape to the fabric, pinning the patterns right side up onto the right side of the fabric. Match the grain line marked to the grain of the fabric wherever possible. Note that there will be times you will want to ignore the grain to take advantage of a particular pattern or motif. Cut out each piece with an exact 4 mm [⅛"] seam allowance all around, *except for the parts marked with a zigzag line* (i.e. the parts that will underlap) which should have a 1 cm [⅜"] seam allowance. Cutting the seam allowance as precisely as possible is very important for applique. Keep the fabric pieces pinned to paper patterns.

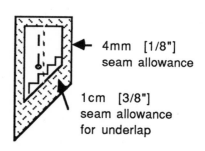

4mm [1/8"] seam allowance

1cm [3/8"] seam allowance for underlap

• This step is optional but is best taken by those with little applique experience. Making an exact 4 mm [⅛″] seam, tack (baste) all the seam allowances into place, except where an underlap is indicated, in which case, the seam allowance is just left flat. Use your fingers to press the seam allowance into place. Fingers are preferable to an iron, because an iron can often create more problems than it solves. Make nicks in the seam allowances only if absolutely necessary for concave or V-shapes. Your applique pieces should now be exactly the same shapes as your paper patterns, except for the underlaps. Pin the paper patterns back into place on each prepared fabric shape.

• Assemble your applique design in its correct place onto the background fabric. Each piece of applique should have its own piece of tracing paper pattern still pinned in place.

The paper pieces should fit back together again to make the design, with the underlaps all tucking neatly beneath the pieces which will overlap them. Carefully pin the pieces in place.

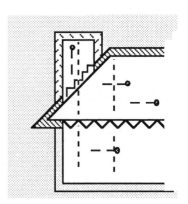

• Tack the pieces to the background and remove the tracing paper patterns.

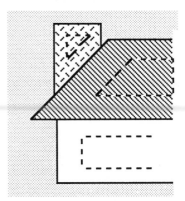

• Applique the pieces in place, using a coloured thread that matches the piece to be appliqued. If you have already tacked the seam allowances in place, then the pieces can be stitched as they are. If the seam allowances have not been tacked, then you will need to turn under the seam allowances of 4 mm [⅛″] as you stitch. Use the needle to help you smoothly turn the seam allowance under, especially on curves. Make nicks in the seam allowances for concave curves and V-shapes, but keep the nicks to a minimum.

To make the stitching almost invisible, bring the needle out from the fold in the seam allowance, then straight down into the background, coming back up again into the fold with the next stitch, and so on.

First sew the pieces that are beneath overlapping pieces, then sew the top pieces.

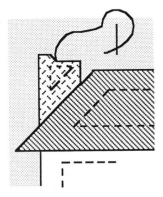

• Cut out patterns for decorative details such as eyes. Prepare these as necessary (see below) and stitch into place.

Special situations

Circles

Exact circles of all sizes can be made following this method.

• Cut a circle of cardboard the exact size you want the circle to be. Cut out the fabric with an approximately 1 cm [⅜″] seam allowance all around.
• Hand sew a small running stitch around the fabric circle about 4 mm [⅛″] from the edge.

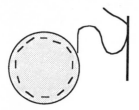

• Place the cardboard circle in the centre of the fabric circle, and draw up the running stitch, gathering the fabric as tightly as possible around the cardboard. Press firmly with a steam iron.

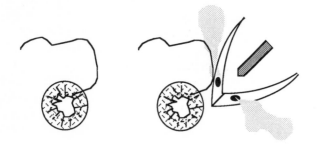

• Loosen the stitching and remove the cardboard circle. Trim the seam allowance back to 4 mm [⅛″] with sharp scissors.

• Fold the pressed seam allowance under and applique the prepared circle in place.

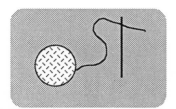

Sharp points

Sharp points can be sewn by folding in three stages. First fold down the seam allowance up to the point, then fold over the tip of the point, and finally fold down the seam allowance on the other side of the point.

Narrow strips

To make narrow strips, cut pieces as bias strips the required width and length, with seam allowances. These pieces can be curved as needed. Do not worry about matching grain in this situation. Extremely narrow strips are best made by making rouleau (see below).

Rouleau

To make rouleau, cut strips of fabric on the bias 3 cm [1¼″] wide. Fold the strips in half lengthwise, right sides inside, and machine stitch down at the required width. Trim away the seam allowance to make a narrow seam, and turn rouleau right side out using a loop turner, or a bodkin (with a strong thread knotted to it).

Machine applique

Machine appliqued pieces should sit flat and smooth. the satin stitch should be even, and the background remain unpuckered. Machine applique for a quilt also should be soft, so the method I am suggesting does not involve any fusing of fabrics, which can make the fabric stiff and bubble after washing. The method involves working from a paper design placed on the *wrong* side of the background fabric. Then, working from the wrong side, the patches are applied in sequence to the right side with a running stitch. The applique is then completed by satin stitch worked on the right side. While this method is ideal for quilts, it also can be used successfully for all machine applique.

Some special requirements are needed for machine applique:

Stabiliser

To prevent the fabrics puckering and stretching while you are sewing them, machine applique must be backed with some kind of stabiliser while you are working. After the applique is finished, the stabiliser is torn away. The stabiliser can be paper (lining paper for wall paper is ideal because it has a slightly rough surface), or some kind of vilene product (non-woven stiffening). There are now some products specially made for this purpose (such as 'Sew and Tear'). Your fabric or handicraft shop should be able to advise you on these products.

Pins

Pins are used to hold the fabric in place for the first row of stitching in machine applique. Use ordinary dressmakers pins, not the berry pins, so that the heads do not get in the way.

Threads

While normal dressmaking threads can be used for machine applique, a smoother more even satin stitch can be obtained from threads specially made for machine embroidery. Some of these threads give a sheen to the satin stitch.

The process of machine applique

• Using an ordinary pencil, trace your design onto your paper or other stabilser (hereafter this will be called the paper). This can be done by taping the design and the paper against a well lit window. The tracing needs to be a *reverse* image of the design, so place the right side of the design against the window. Draw a grain line down the centre of the design.

• Study the design to analyse in which order the fabrics should be applied, and number each part of the design accordingly. For instance, give the number one to the parts of the design where the bottom layer of fabric is to be put, number two to the parts where the next fabric goes, and so on.

• Place background fabric right side down, and pin traced design on top, with the design facing up. Make sure the grain line of the background fabric matches the vertical line on the design. Pin lightly around outer edge.

• Select the fabric for the first layer in the design, (the fabric which will be applied to the areas you have labelled with a number one). Cut the shapes required, making each piece at least 1 cm [½"] larger all around. Several areas can be covered by one piece of fabric, if appropriate.

• Working from the *fabric side* pin the applique patch in place with pins at each corner, pinning through all layers (use ordinary dressmakers pins). You may need to hold the design up to the window to pin the patch in the right place.

• Turn over to the *paper side* and pin at right angles to the design lines, pinning frequently and putting the heads of the pins to the centre of the shape. Pin through all layers.

• Thread the bobbin with colour to match the applique patch, and set the machine for straight stitching, at length between 1½ and 2. Working from the *paper side*, slowly stitch around the traced line on the paper design, stitching carefully across the pins. Begin and end in the middle of the one side of the shape, not at a corner.

• Turn to *fabric side*, and using a sharp pair of scissors, trim away excess fabric from the applique patch, trimming close to the machine stitching.

• Repeat this process with all the fabrics neded for the applique. *Do not tear away the paper yet.*

• Set machine to satin stitch, and do some trial samples to get the satin stitches even and smooth. Working on the *fabric side*, satin stitch around each shape, matching both top and bobbin thread to the colour required. Again, work the stitching in the order that the patches were applied so that the seam ends are neatly covered. Bring loose ends to the back and tie off. Complete any extra machine embroidery required at this stage.

• Remove paper from the back of the design and press.

Special situations

Long narrow bits can be made by making a rouleau to the desired width and length. Press the rouleau flat with the seam to the underneath. Pin or tack to your design and stitch down with two rows of small straight stitching. When making a curve, press the seam on the rouleau to one side of the underneath. Place the seam side of the rouleau towards the inner side of the curve, as it will have less stretch than the other side.

Transparent fabrics need to have any applique patches beneath them well trimmed so that they do not show through unnecessarily.

Embroidery stitches

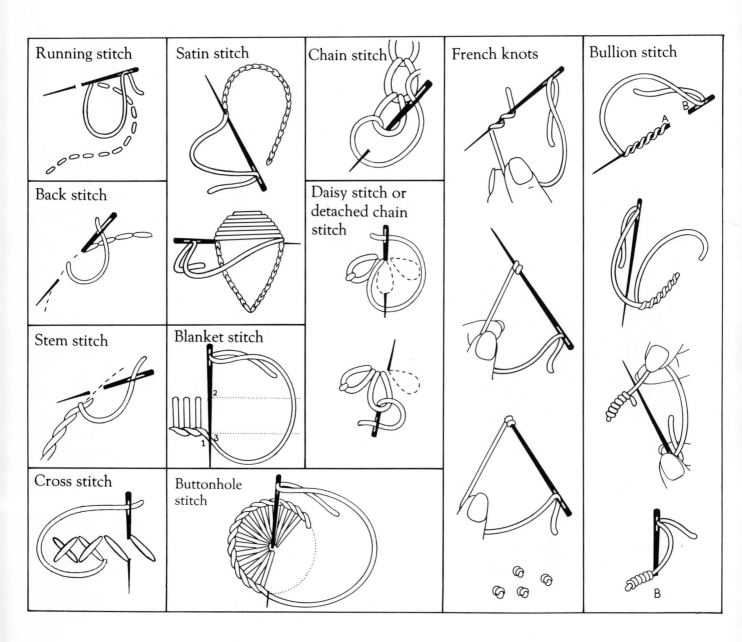

Running stitch

Satin stitch

Chain stitch

French knots

Bullion stitch

Back stitch

Daisy stitch or detached chain stitch

Stem stitch

Blanket stitch

Cross stitch

Buttonhole stitch

Quilting

Tying

The easiest way of joining the three layers of a quilt together is by tying. Tying is also used in conjunction with strip quilting, to hold the backing of the quilt in place. The tying can be made nearly invisible by tying the knots on the back of the quilt, or can be made a feature of the quilt by using wool, and making bows on the top of the quilt. Ribbon bows could also be sewn to the ties, or buttons could be stitched on. Prepare the layers for tying by pinning the backing, batting and top of the quilt together.

• Thread a suitably sized needle with a piece of the thread chosen. Use either a strong thread (such as quilting thread) doubled, or wool.

• Starting from the side of the quilt where the knot will be, push the needle straight through the quilt layers. Pull the thread through, but leave enough thread behind to comfortably tie a knot (longer if for a bow). Taking only a tiny stitch, push the needle back through the quilt.

• Repeat, going through the quilt in the same places as the first stitch.

• Tie the ends off into a firm reef knot. Trim ends, leaving 6 mm [¼″] ends (if you trim too closely, the knot will undo). Add a bow after the reef knot if a bow is desired.

• Repeat ties across the quilt. A big quilt will need to be rolled up as you work across it.

Hand quilting

The running stitch in hand quilting makes a gentle broken line. The quilting compresses the three layers of the quilt sandwich together along the lines of stitching which creates a shadow, while the light catches the unquilted areas. It is the effect of the light and shadow which really forms a quilting pattern.

Quilting requires some special equipment; a quilting hoop or frame, a between needle, quilting thread, and at least one thimble.

Designs for quilting

• *Outline quilting*. The simplest approach to quilting is to outline the patchwork shapes. This is most appropriate for the birds and animals, as it makes them stand out in *bas relief*. The quilting is done 'in the ditch', (i.e. as close as possible to the seam line) and no marking is necessary.

• *Lines and grids*. Simple straight lines and variations of these, such as lines at differing distances apart, or lines crossing to form squares and diamonds, always make good quilting patterns. They are simple to mark and sew.

• *Echo quilting*. Lines of quilting can echo the patchwork or applique shapes. This can be a very effective way of quilting a background.

• *Motifs and designs*. There are many beautiful designs available for quilting, such as the traditional wreath and twist patterns. Any kind of motif can be used, hearts, flowers, butterflies, balloons, ducks, teddy bears, or anything else. Geometric patterns of all types, such as triangles, circles and interlocking squares, are very suitable for background areas. Lines or shapes in your patchwork can often suggest designs.

• *Free quilting.* Quilting in a pattern which develops as you go. Generally it is best to begin with a sketch plan of how you want the overall look to be, then work it out from there as you stitch.

Marking the quilting designs

• Marking with a pencil. Marking for quilting is generally done before the layers of the quilt are joined. Spread the quilt top onto a hard flat surface. With a very sharp pencil mark as *lightly* as you can; just enough to follow the lines. Lines can be drawn with a ruler, or drawn around cardboard or plastic templates. If you have access to a light box, you can trace the patterns onto the quilt. Taping the quilt to a brightly lit window is possible, but usually awkward.

• Marking with masking tape. This is done after the layers of the quilt are joined together. It is most suitable for straight lines, but the tape can be snipped to make it bend around corners, or else narrow tape can be used. Place the tape on the prepared quilt just before you begin to stitch. Quilt along side the tape, then remove the tape to the next line. The tape can be used several times before it loses its stickiness. Masking tape is particularly useful for marking parallel lines, or across squares or other regular shapes. Do not leave the tape on the quilt when you are not working on it, to avoid any residue of the tape remaining on the quilt.

Preparation for hand quilting

• Careful preparation is one of the secrets of successful quilting. The three layers of the quilt must be smoothly tacked (basted) together, with no wrinkles in any of the layers. A quilting hoop or frame should be used to hold the three layers of the quilt smoothly in place while you quilt. However, some people prefer not to have a hoop or frame and quilt small pieces in their lap.

• Press the patchwork top thoroughly. Use a sharp pencil to mark any quilting lines or motifs required.

• Prepare a backing fabric. Join lengths of fabric together, if necessary, to make the size you need. Press the backing. Make the backing about 5 cm [2″] larger than the patchwork top. Use a soft fabric which is easy to sew, such as a lawn. Plain fabrics will show up your quilting more than prints.

• Cut the piece of batting the same size as the backing fabric. For larger quilts, the batting may need to be joined. Butt the cut edges of the batting together, and loosely stitch by hand, using a whip stitch.

• Lay the fabric backing down, right side down, onto a large flat surface. Smooth the batting over the backing, then lay the patchwork on top, right side up. Make sure that there are no wrinkles in any of the layers.

• Pin the three layers together, placing pins about 10–15 cm [4–6″] apart. Use a long needle and large stitches to tack (baste) the three layers together. Tack in a grid, with lines of stitching about 10–15 cm [4–6″] apart.

• Lay the inner ring of your quilting hoop down, smooth the prepared quilt on top, then push on the outer ring of the hoop, tightening the ring as necessary. The quilt should not be drum tight, but should have a little slackness in it. The three layers should now be held smoothly in place, ready for quilting. Always begin quilting in the centre of your quilt, and move methodically from quilted to unquilted parts.

The process of hand quilting

• Thread a 'between' needle (size 8 or 9 is usually comfortable) with quilting thread, making the thread no longer than 45 cm [18″]. Tie a knot at the end of the thread.

• Put a thimble on the middle finger of your sewing hand, and, if you wish, protect the index finger of your other hand with another thimble. Rest the hoop comfortably on a table or on the arms of a chair so that both your hands are free.

• Begin the quilting by pushing your needle up through the quilt at the place where you want to start. Tug gently on the thread to pull the knot through the backing and into the batting. Make a small back stitch to anchor the thread firmly in place.

• With your index finger just below where you are stitching, push the needle through the quilt so that the tip of the needle just grazes the top of the finger (or thimble) underneath. Rock the point of the needle upwards, and bring it out so that you have made a small stitch. Your thimble should be behind the needle, pushing it. With practice, you will find that you will soon be able to make more than one stitch at a time. The stitching must go through all three layers, hence the need to protect the index finger below the quilt. Continue quilting in this manner, following the marked lines or design you have chosen. Sometimes you will have to quilt through seam allowances which will make the stitching difficult. If it becomes impossible to make a stitch in one motion, be content to stab stitch — in other words, to push the needle down through the quilt in one motion, and back up again in a second motion.

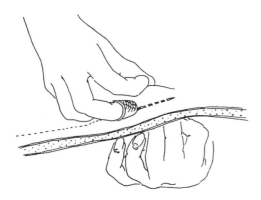

• To end the quilting, make a stab stitch straight down, going through all layers. Then, in a second motion, come back up through and split the last stitch you have made. Next, go back down through the end of your last stitch, but only through into the batting layer. Take a long stitch through the batting and bring the thread out to the top and snip it off.

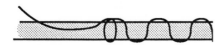

The process of machine quilting

Machine quilting makes a stronger unbroken line than hand quilting, and also compresses the layers of a quilt more firmly. The effect of machine quilting will not be the same as hand quilting, but it still is very suitable for lots of projects because of its speed and strength.

The secret of successful machine quilting is having the three layers move smoothly through the machine together, without one of the fabrics being pushed ahead of the others.

The major difficulty with machine quilting is to get a sewing machine to handle the bulk of the quilt beneath the space of the sewing machine arm. Machine quilting, therefore, is most suitable for small projects such as cot quilts, cushions, clothing and bags. It is possible to quilt large quilts by either quilting them in sections which are later joined, or by quilting in straight line patterns which go from one side of the quilt to the other (the quilt can be rolled up to move through the arm of the machine).

Threads used for dressmaking are generally suitable for machine quilting, and because they come in a wide range of colours, the colour can be matched to your patchwork. If you cannot find an exact match, choose a colour a shade darker. An invisible thread can also be used for machine quilting as it blends into all colours, but use it on the top of the machine only, so that snarls do not occur. The bobbin thread should match the colour of the quilt backing.

While it is preferable to have a soft backing fabric for hand quilting, a firmer fabric is desirable for machine quilting.

• Set up your machine and a space around it ready for machine quilting. It is most important that you have a large area clear to the left and behind the machine. Attach the machine foot which is most suitable for machine quilting, and turn on the dual feed mechanism if it is available.

• Prepare the quilt layers in the manner described above for hand quilting, but instead of tacking (basting) the layers together, it is only necessary to pin them. Avoid placing pins across intended quilting lines.

• Thread the machine with a colour to match the patchwork on the top, and a colour to match the backing on the bobbin. Set the stitch length to around 2½ or 3.

• If you are quilting a whole quilt in a pattern of straight lines from side to side, roll it up from both ends to expose only the first line to be sewn at the centre of the quilt.

• Stitch 'in the ditch' of the seam line, or along lines you have marked for a quilting design. When you are stitching in the ditch, it will be easiest to sew along the side away from the seam allowances.

Begin and end your stitching with a couple of back stitches, and trim thread ends neatly.

Use the fingers of one hand to spread the quilt sideways either side of the needle as you stitch. Use the other hand underneath your work to smoothly feed it through the machine. If you have to stop stitching in the middle of a line, always stop with the needle down so that the line stays straight.

• If you are quilting a whole quilt, roll and reroll the quilt ready for each seam. When all the lines in one direction are done, turn the quilt and roll it so that it is ready to quilt in the opposite direction.

Joining pre-quilted sections

If you are machine quilting a large quilt in sections, joint the pieces together in either of two ways:

Method 1 If the quilting lines go to the edge of the sections, join all layers together, with seams on the back of the quilt. Trim away excess batting and seam allowances. Cover the seams with fabric strips.

Prepare strips of fabric, (cut on the straight of the grain) double the width required to cover the trimmed seam allowances. Press both sides of the strip into the centre along its length. Pin the prepared strips over the seam, making sure you enclose all the seam allowances. Hand stitch the strips in place.

Method 2 If the quilting lines are at least 2.5 cm [1″] away from the edge of the quilted sections, stitch only 5 of the layers together into a seam, leaving one side of the backing free. Trim away excess batting and finger press seam allowances to one side. Fold under a seam allowance on the backing fabric which has not been included in the seam, and hand stitch it along the seam line.

Strip quilting

Strip quilting is a type of machine quilting in which pieces of fabric are pieced and quilted at the same time. It is a one step way to quick and easy patchwork. Log cabin patchwork can be successfully sewn by this method.

It is generally preferable to use thin firm batting for strip quilting as the softer batting can be difficult to work with.

The completed strip quilted blocks are joined together and then a backing is put onto the whole quilt. Binding the edges and placing ties in the corners between the blocks will be sufficient to hold all the layers together.

Strip quilting a block

• Cut the prewashed and pressed fabrics into strips; the rotary cutter makes quick work of this. Press the strips to remove creases from folding.

• Cut the batting 2.5 cm [1″] larger than the block or area you are strip quilting.

• Lay your *first* strip of fabric down onto the batting, with *right side up*.

• Lay your *second* strip on top of the first, *right side down*, and pin in place. Machine down the edge of the strips, making an even 6 mm [¼″] seam). Remove the pins and fold back the top strip and finger press the seam flat. Do not use an iron, it would flatten the batting.

• Lay your *third strip, right side down, on top of the second strip*, and pin and stitch as before. Continue in this manner until the required number of strips are stitched into place.

• Machine close (2 mm [1/16″]) to the edges of the strip quilted piece. Alternatively, pin a pattern of the shape of the block or another design onto the piece and machine stitch around the edges of this pattern. Trim back to the stitching.

Strip quilting the log cabin

Proceed as for strip quilting above, but begin in the centre of your block with a square, placed right side up. The first strip is laid over this, right side down, then pinned and stitched into place.

Rotate the block and lay the next strip over the second side of the centre square, pin and stitch in place. Continue in this manner until strips have been applied to all sides of the centre square. Repeat this process until the block is completed. Straight stitch closely around the outside edges to complete the block.

Talking Point quilt: this traditional style quilt with its
cheerful colours makes learning fun (p 34).
Created by Wendy Saclier

Teddy Bear log cabin quilt: the centre motifs in each rectangle make a delightful variation on this cot quilt (p 36). Made by Judy Turner

Quilt and cushion construction

Making a quilt

First, determine what size you want the finished quilt to be. If the quilt is to fit a certain bed, measure the bed and the amount of overhang you want. The size of a quilt can be varied by:

- increasing or decreasing the number of blocks
- changing the width of the border or borders
- varying the width of the sashing (if the quilt has sashing)
- changing the size of the blocks.

Plan to make your quilt a little larger than the size required, as quilting will take up some of the size. Hand quilting can take up about 2.5 cm [1″], and machine quilting much more than this. If a quilt must be an exact size choose a design with an outside border which can be trimmed back to size after the quilting is finished.

Next, choose the patchwork or applique designs that you want to use and decide how you want to use them. Patchwork quilts made from blocks (whether geometric or pictorial pieced blocks, or applique blocks) can be varied in lots of different ways:

- the blocks can be set next to each other (Advent Calendar quilt)
- the blocks can be reversed (Elephant quilt)
- the blocks can be varied in size (Benjamin Bunny quilt
- the blocks can be set with strips between (Miss Mouse quilt)
- the blocks can be given borders (Alphabet quilt, see the pieced alphabet blocks)
- the blocks can be set with patchwork designs in the strips (Teddy bear, Teddy bear)
- pictorial blocks can be alternated with geometric blocks (Zoo quilt)
- pieced or applique blocks can be alternated with plain blocks (Basket quilt)
- the blocks can be set together to make a picture (Farm Life quilt)
- the blocks can be used to make a medallion style quilt in which a centre is framed by successive borders (Panda quilt).

It is a good idea to begin with a simple plan on paper. You may well want to vary it as you go, but the plan helps you get started.

Steps to be followed

- Make the necessary templates.
- Estimate the amount of fabric you will need:

Top of quilt. First measure any borders which might need to be cut the length of the fabric. Work out how many times each template shape will be repeated. See how many times the template shape (including seam allowances) will fit across the width of the fabric once any borders have been allowed for. Then calculate how many rows will be required to cut the number of shapes needed. For the pictorial blocks you will generally only require small amounts of fabric to make the animals. The size of the block plus seam allowances is usually sufficient, and will give you enough fabric to make pieces the whole length or width of the block.

Note that all quantities of fabric suggested in

this book refer to fabric 114 cm [45″] wide.

Batting. The size of your finished patchwork top, plus 5 cm [2″] all around.

Backing fabric. The same size as your finished patchwork top, plus 5 cm [2″] all around. Lengths of fabric may have to be joined to make the size required.

• Choose and purchase your fabrics. When you are buying the fabrics, group the rolls of fabric together to see how the colours interact with one another. Carry samples of your fabrics around with you to match and coordinate colours. Remember to have a variety in the tones (the lightness and darkness) of the colours you choose.

• Prewash and press the fabrics.

• Cut out pieces for the quilt, either by marking and cutting with scissors, or by using the rotary cutter and ruler.

• Stitch the patchwork pieces or blocks together. Follow the piecing order carefully for the pictorial blocks.

• Construct the centre of the quilt front, adding sashings according to your plan.

• Add borders. Always measure the length of the borders from the finished patchwork top,

measuring along the middle of quilt, both crosswise and lengthwise. Be flexible, sometimes fabrics you have originally chosen for borders do not look so good when you actually see the patchwork finished, so check before you stitch them on. Some borders need to have mitred corners, which means that the two pieces are joined at a 45° angle. When sewing a mitre, it is important to only sew on the seam line, and not across the seam allowances. Mark the 45° angle with a setsquare.

How to mitre a corner for a quilt border.

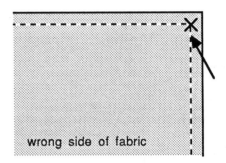

1. Mark point on corner where the seam lines will cross.

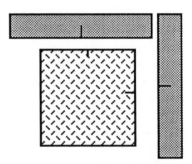

2. Cut out borders length required, and mark centres with a pin. Mark centre of quilt top.

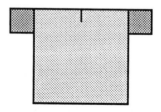

3. Pin border to quilt top, matching marking pins.

Adding sashing and borders.

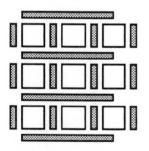

1. Blocks and sashing strips.

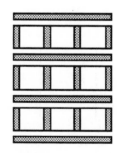

2. Join blocks to short strips to make rows.

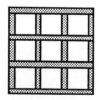

3. Join rows to long strips.

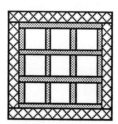

4. Add border.

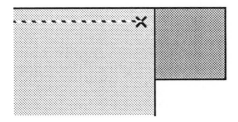

4. Stitch border to quilt, stitching only to marked point, and then backtracking to finish. Repeat step 3 and 4 with second border.

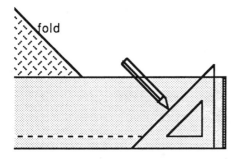

5. Fold quilt into corner so the two border strips become parallel. Mark a 45° angle from point where stitching ends. Pin. Stitch on this line, sewing only to corner point.

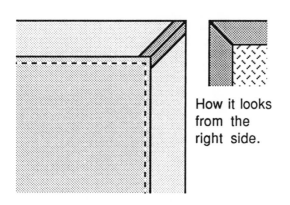

How it looks from the right side.

6. Trim and press seam allowances open.

• Press quilt top well, and mark any quilting designs needed. Prepare the backing and batting for quilting. Pin and tack (baste) the three layers together.

• Quilt by hand or machine. The quilt is easier to bind if the outside edge is finished with a row of straight stitching just 2 mm [1/16″] from the cut edges of the quilt top (note that this is outside the seam line). Trim excess batting and backing to the width you want the final binding to be, (this ensures that the binding is not unfilled and flabby).

• Finish the edges of the quilt by either binding the edges with strips or by folding the top of the quilt to the back:

Method 1 Binding the edges with strips of fabric.

Bias strips are necessary if you need to curve around the corners, otherwise the strips can be cut on the straight grain. Measure your quilt across the middle both lengthwise and crosswise, and prepare the strips to these lengths adding enough to tuck in neatly over the binding at each end. Measuring the quilt through the centre is more accurate than measuring the sides which may have become stretched. These middle measurements must be used to make your quilt sit flat and straight when completed. Strips will often need to be joined together to make the length required.

Strips of fabric folded double make a neat and strong binding, and this is recommended for most of the quilts. Cut the strips four times the width required for the finished binding, plus 1.2 cm [1/2″] for seam allowances. Strips cut 8 cm [3″] are a useful size, and result in a binding about 1.5 cm [5/8″] wide.

Attach the binding by pinning the strips to the right side of the edge of the quilt, aligning the raw edges of the strips with the edge of the quilt top. Machine stitch in place. Fold the strips to the back of the quilt, tucking the ends neatly over the corners. Hand stitch strips to the back of the quilt.

Method 2 Bringing the top of the quilt to the back. Trim batting and backing to the final quilt size. Fold the top of the quilt to the back, turn under a small seam allowance, and hand stitch in place. Note that when using this method, extra fabric needs to be added to the final border of the patchwork top so that there will be sufficient to fold over to the back.

Alternatively, bias binding, can be sewn to the top of the quilt, stitching through all layers. Trim away excess batting, then fold the edge of the quilt so that the bias binding lies flat on the back of the quilt. Pin and hand stitch in place. The bias can either be purchased (1.2 cm [1/2″] wide after the seam allowances are pressed down), or made to match the back of the quilt by using bias cut strips of the backing fabric.

Making bias strips.

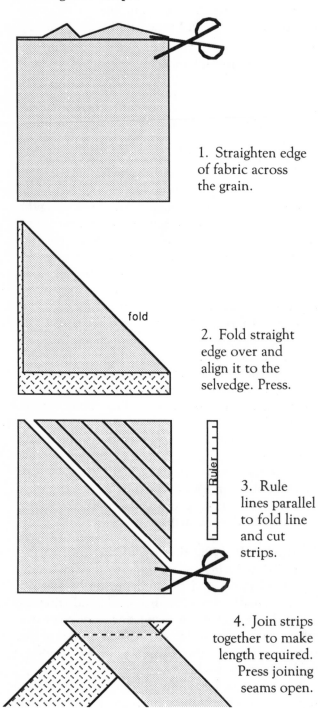

1. Straighten edge of fabric across the grain.

2. Fold straight edge over and align it to the selvedge. Press.

fold

3. Rule lines parallel to fold line and cut strips.

Ruler

4. Join strips together to make length required. Press joining seams open.

Making cushions

Exact requirements cannot be given because cushion sizes vary. However, the following is a guide, based on a 40 cm [16"] cushion. You will need:

• finished block of patchwork, plus borders, made to size required;

• batting, size of patchwork block plus 2.5 cm [1"] all around (about 50 cm [20"] square);

• backing fabric for quilting, same size as batting;

• fabric for back of cushion plus binding (about 50 cm [20"]). You will need a piece of fabric the size of the cushion plus an extra 5 cm [2"] in length to allow for zip insertion;

• zip, 5 cm [2"] shorter than the width of the cushion.

• Assemble the top. Tack (baste) the backing, batting and patchwork front together and quilt. Sew a line of straight stitching close to the edge of the patchwork top (note that this line is outside the seam allowance, only 2 mm [1/16"] from cut edge). Trim excess away from stitching.

• Cut a rectangle of fabric for the cushion back, the same width as the cushion top, but 5 cm [2"] longer for seam allowances for the zip. Insert the zipper across the centre of the back.

• Cut bias strips 4 cm [1½"] wide from fabric for binding . Join strips together to make length required (4 times the width of the cushion, about 2 m [2 yd]).

• Pin cushion front and back wrong sides together. Pin bias strip to the front edge right sides together. Round the corners gently and tuck ends in neatly. Trim.   Stitch bias around cushion.

• Finger press a small seam allowance on the bias strip. Roll it over to the back of the cushion and hand stitch it in place.

II

Patterns and projects

Measurement

All dimensions are given in both the metric and imperial measurements, the latter being marked by square brackets, e.g. [1″]. Note that the two systems *are not interchangeable* as only whole figure equivalents have been used. Use only one system in any one project, as the measurements for each project have been worked out independently for both systems to enable simple multiples to be used. Templates, block and border sizes are all given *without seam allowances added*. The only exceptions to this are the measurements given for cutting binding strips which all include seam allowances. All other measurements need to have seams added.

Simple squares

Quick and easy to make, these quilts are ideal for gifts.
If you use a rotary cutter to cut out the squares,
you will be amazed how soon the quilt will be ready to sew.
Piece with automatic seam allowances.

Tied bassinet quilt

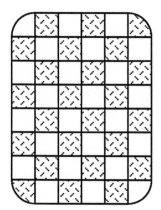

Finished size

64 × 48 cm [24 × 18″] not including binding.
8 rows of 6 squares each 8 cm [3″].

Requirements

• Fabric A 30 cm [12″] for 24 squares.
• Fabric B 50 cm [20″] for 24 squares and binding.
• Batting 70 × 54 cm [26 × 20″].
• Backing fabric 70 × 54 cm [26 × 20″].
• Wool for ties 9 m [10 yd].

Template pattern

Add seam allowances

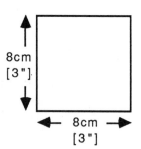

8cm
[3″]

8cm
[3″]

Cut out

• Fabric A, 24 squares.
• Fabric B, bias strips for binding 6 cm [2½″] wide and 24 squares.

Construction

• Join squares into rows, alternating prints. Make 8 rows of 6 squares each.
• Assemble quilt layers. Cut wool into 24 cm [9″] lengths and use to tie at junctions, finishing with bows.
• Straight stitch close to edges and trim excess batting and backing.
• Bind quilt with bias strips, rounding the corners and folding the ends in neatly, making a double binding.

Machine quilted cot quilt

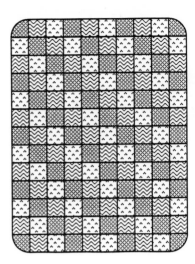

Template pattern

Add seam allowances

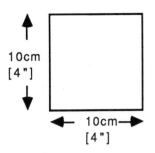

10cm
[4"]

10cm
[4"]

Cut out

- Dark print, 44 squares and strips for bias binding 6 cm [2¼"] wide.
- Medium print, 43 squares.
- Light print, 43 squares.

Finished size

130 × 100 cm [52 × 40"] not including binding. 13 rows of 10 squares each 10 cm [4"].

Requirements

- Print fabric, dark tone 1.1 m [1¼ yd] for squares and binding.
- Print fabric, medium tone 80 cm [¾ yd].
- Print fabric, light tone 80 cm [¾ yd].
- Batting 140 × 120 cm [56 × 44"].
- Backing fabric 1.4 m [1¾ yd].

Construction

- Join squares into rows, arranging prints on diagonal, as in diagram. Make 13 rows of 10 squares each.
- Assemble quilt layers and machine quilt in ditch between rows, both lengthwise and crosswise.
- Straight stitch close to the edges of the quilt. Trim away excess batting and backing.
- Bind quilt with joined bias strips, rounding corners and folding the ends in neatly to make a double binding.

Talking Point Quilt
'And where is the white cat?'

This quilt gains its title 'Talking Point Quilt' because it can be the basis of lots of games that stimulate the development of speech. Where is the white cat? Where is the pink elephant? Can you find another elephant? And so on. Collect lots of small pieces of prints with motifs on them; ask your family and friends to contribute. The quilt is simply made from one regular shape, a right angle triangle. It can be pieced with automatic seam allowances. Designed and created by Wendy Saclier.

Finished size

134 × 106 cm [52½ × 41½"] not including binding.

Requirements

• Quantity of small fabric scraps with printed motifs, half light in colour, half dark (including red prints) for triangles and binding. Total amount required approximately 80 cm [1 yd] each light and dark.
• Blue fabric for inside border, 30 cm [12"]
• Red fabric for outside border, 70 cm [¾ yd]
• Batting 150 × 120 cm [57 × 46"]
• Backing fabric 1.5 m [1¾ yd]

Template patterns

Add seam allowances

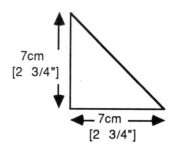

7cm
[2 3/4"]

7cm
[2 3/4"]

Light and dark triangle joined to make square.

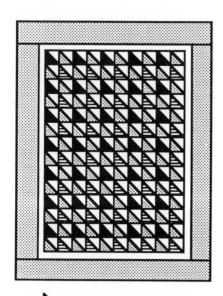

Red print triangles.

Cut out

- Light print, 140 triangles.
- Dark print, 140 triangles (35 red print).
- Blue fabric strips for inside border 4 cm [1½"] wide (plus seams).
- Red fabric strips for outside border 14 cm [5½"] wide (plus seams).
- Strips of printed fabric (straight grain) for binding. Cut 8 cm [3"] wide.

Construction

- Piece triangles into squares; one light and one dark together.
- Join squares into rows, 14 rows of 10 squares each. Distribute red print triangles evenly by placing them at every second place in each alternate row as illustrated.
- Add border of blue, then red outside border.
- Mark quilting motifs onto border. Use silhouette outlines of shapes such as a duck, teddy bear, rabbit, bird, etc. Add words such as 'and where is the white cat?'
- Assemble quilt layers. Outline quilt triangles and borders. Quilt marked motifs.
- Bind edges of quilt with strips made from short lengths of print fabrics joined together, making a double binding.

Teddy Bear Log Cabin Quilt

This quilt is made in the traditional pattern known as the log cabin. It is given a delightful twist by using printed motifs as the centre squares. Find a fabric with an attractive print, and use this as the basis of your quilt; the colours in the printed motif can be echoed in the strips.

The quilt is especially quick and easy to make as it is strip quilted, so the quilting is done as you sew the pieces together.

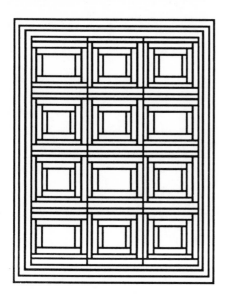

Finished size

115 × 90 cm [46 × 36″]
4 × 3 blocks each 25 cm [10″] and three narrow borders.

Requirements

Exact requirements cannot be given, because your choice of fabric for the centre squares and strips will determine how much fabric you need. The dimensions given for the quilt illustrated can easily be varied to suit the fabrics you choose.

• Length of printed fabric sufficient to give 12 motifs.

• Assortment of fabrics to make strips, borders, and bindings; approximately 3 m [3¼ yd] in all.

• Thin batting 2.3 m [2½ yd], 73 cm [28″] wide.

• Backing fabric 1.3 m [1½ yd].

Cut out

Use these dimensions as a guide, making adaptations for the fabrics of your choice.

• Fabric for blocks 25 cm [10″] square. First cut rectangles with motif for centres. Cut either 10 cm [4″] square or 10 × 15 cm [4 × 6″] plus seams. Next cut strips 2.5 cm [1″] wide (plus seams).

- Border strips (straight grain) 2.5 cm [1"] wide, (plus seams) for 3 borders.
- Batting squares. Cut 12 each 28 cm [11"] square.
- Batting strips for borders. 4 strips 10 × 120 cm [4 × 48"].
- Strips of straight grain fabric for binding 6 cm [2½"] wide.

Construction

- Construct log cabin blocks. Pin square of fabric with motif to middle of the batting square. Sew strips log cabin fashion (courthouse step variation) to complete block. Straight stitch close to edge of block, and trim away excess batting. Make 12 blocks.
- Stitch blocks together to make centre of quilt, 4 rows of 3 blocks.
- Strip quilt 3 border strips to each batting strip. Straight stitch close to lengthwise edges and trim. Pin borders to quilt and stitch in place. Mitre the corners. Using only tip of iron, and pressing very lightly, run iron down seams between blocks.
- Pin backing fabric to quilt top. Tie at all block junctions, putting knots at the back of the quilt.
- Bind quilt with strips (straight grain) making a double thickness binding.

Football Stripes Quilt and cushions for sports fans

Make a quilt in the colours of a favourite team. The quilt is very quick and easy to make by strip quilting.

Finished size

200 × 120 cm [80 × 48″] approx.
10 × 6 blocks each 20 cm [8″] approx.

Requirements

• Fabric amounts for this quilt will vary with the number of colours chosen and the size of the strips. Use the following guide.

• Each strip 5 cm [2″] wide needs 90 cm [1 yd] fabric for whole quilt.

• Each strip 2.5 cm [1″] wide needs 60 cm [¾ yd] fabric for whole quilt.

• Extra fabric 50 cm [20″] to make strips for binding.

• Batting suitable for strip quilting (thin and firm), 5 m [5½ yd] of 73 cm [28″] width.

• Backing fabric 2.6 m [3 yd].

(The quilt illustrated was made with two lots of 5 cm [2″] strips in green and four lots of 2.5 cm [1″] strips yellow, blue and two white.)

Cut out

• Strips in appropriate colours and widths, adding 1.2 cm [½″] to each strip for seam allowances.

• Batting rectangles cut 115 × 24 cm [45 × 9″].

• Strips (straight grain) for binding 6 cm [2½″] wide.

Variations

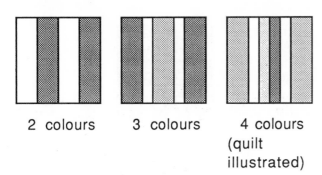

2 colours   3 colours   4 colours
(quilt
illustrated)

Construction

• Cut batting into rectangles 24 cm [9"] wide and 115 cm [45"] long.

• Cut fabric into strips across the fabric, selvedge to selvedge. Remember to add seam allowances to strip widths. Press strips.

• Strip quilt (see page 28) strips along the length of the batting rectangles, pinning each strip before stitching. Sew strips in the order of the pattern chosen.

• Straight stitch along lengthwise edges of outside strips and trim away excess batting.

• Measure carefully the width of the strip quilted rectangle. Using this measurement, make a template which is exactly this measurement square. (Note that the quilt will not go together correctly unless all your blocks are exactly square.)

• Square off the end of the strip quilted rectangle. Place template over the strip quilting, place ruler on top of template, and use the rotary cutter to cut strip quilting into squares. One rectangle should make 5 squares. Complete 60 blocks in this manner.

• Join blocks together to make quilt. Using only the tip of the iron, and pressing lightly, run the iron down the seams joining blocks.

• Cut backing fabric in half and stitch together to make size required.

• Pin backing to wrong side of front of quilt. Tie quilt at all seam junctions of blocks.

• Bind edges of quilt with straight grain strips to make double binding.

Cushions

Children will not be the only ones who will enjoy these cushions made in bright colours. Quick to make, they are machine pieced from simple shapes. They are machine quilted.

Requirements for one cushion

• Fabric for a 32 cm [12"] square of patchwork.

• Batting 36 cm [14"] square.

• Fabric to back quilting front 36 cm [14"] square.

• Fabric for cushion back 36 × 40 cm [14 × 16"].

• Fabric for bias strips cut 4 cm [1½"] wide to make 1.3 m [1½" yd] total.

• Zipper 25 cm [10"].

Template patterns

Add seam allowances

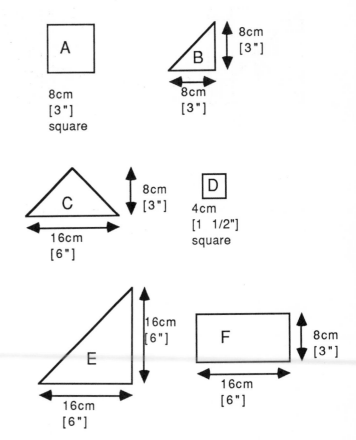

Block size 32 cm [12″]

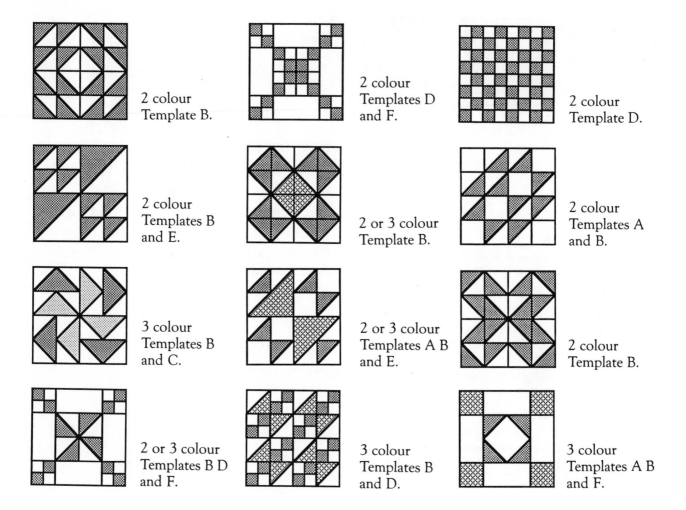

2 colour
Template B.

2 colour
Templates D
and F.

2 colour
Template D.

2 colour
Templates B
and E.

2 or 3 colour
Template B.

2 colour
Templates A
and B.

3 colour
Templates B
and C.

2 or 3 colour
Templates A B
and E.

2 colour
Template B.

2 or 3 colour
Templates B D
and F.

3 colour
Templates B
and D.

3 colour
Templates A B
and F.

Construction

• Make patchwork block by machine piecing with automatic seam allowances.

• Assemble patchwork top, batting and backing. Machine quilt.

• Construct cushion with zipper inserted in back and bias binding to finish the edges (see page 30).

Doll's Quilts

Delight a young lady with an heirloom quilt for her favourite doll. These attractive quilts are made from traditional patchwork block designs. With the exception of the Dresden plate, they are simply pieced from regular shapes. They were created by Elizabeth Russo.

Pinwheel Quilt

Requirements

• Scraps of three blue prints for pinwheels.
• Extra blue print for pinwheels and binding 15 cm [6"].
• Cream fabric for pinwheels 20 cm [8"].
• Batting 40 × 30 cm [14 × 11"].
• Backing fabric 40 × 30 cm [14 × 11"].

Template pattern

Add seam allowances

4 cm [1 1/2"]

4 cm [1 1/2"]

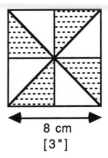

8 cm [3"]

Finished size

32 × 24 cm [12 × 9"] not including binding.
4 × 3 blocks each 8 cm [3"].

Cut out

- 12 triangles from each of four blue prints.
- 48 triangles from cream fabric.
- Binding strips (straight grain) 5.2 cm [2"] wide.

Construction

- Piece 12 pinwheel blocks, 3 blocks of each of the four blue prints.
- Join blocks together into 4 rows of 3 blocks each. Join rows together.
- Assemble quilt layers, and outline quilt pieces.
- Bind edges with strips, making double binding.

Triangle Mosaic Quilt

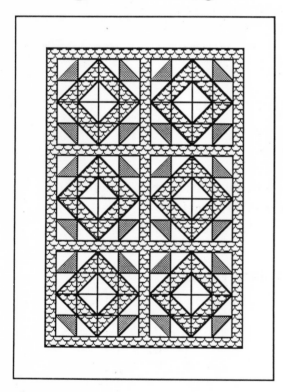

Finished size

68 × 50 cm [26 × 19¼"] not including binding. 3 × 2 blocks each 16 cm [6"] square.

Requirements

- Medium tone print fabric for blocks and sashing, 40 cm [½ yd].

- Dark tone print fabric for blocks and binding, 30 cm [12"].
- Light tone print fabric for blocks and border, 50 cm [20"].
- Batting, 75 × 55 cm [28 × 22"].
- Backing fabric, 75 × 55 cm [28 × 22"].

Template pattern

Add seam allowances

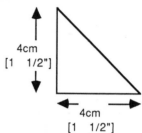

Block design

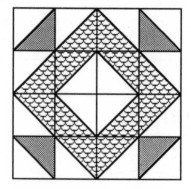

Cut out

- Medium tone fabric 72 triangles, sashing strips 2 cm [¾"] wide plus seams.
- Dark tone fabric 24 triangles, straight grain strips for binding 5.2 cm [2"] wide.
- Light tone fabric 96 triangles, border strips 6 cm [2½"] wide plus seams.

Construction

- Piece triangles into six blocks.
- Add sashing and borders.
- Mark quilting designs on border. Butterfly and flower designs are appropriate motifs.
- Assemble quilt layers, and hand quilt. Outline quilt blocks and sashing, and quilt marked motifs.
- Bind quilt with strips (straight grain).

The prettiest traditional quilts for her favourite dolls (p 41). Created by Elizabeth Russo

Basket Quilt

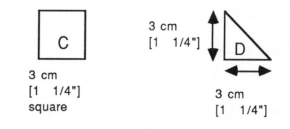

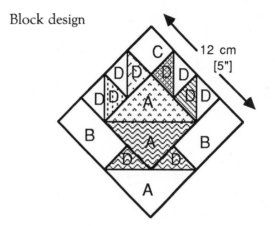

Block design

Template for background is 12 cm [5"] square. Halve this square (across diagonal) for sides, and quarter it for corners.

Finished size

63 × 46 cm [26 × 19"] not including binding.

Requirements

• Scraps of six different prints for triangles in basket.
• White fabric for background in block 20 cm [8"].
• Pale blue fabric for alternate blocks 20 cm [8"].
• Blue fabric for border and binding 40 cm [½ yd].
• Batting 75 × 55 cm [28 × 21"].
• Backing fabric 55 × 70 cm [21 × 28"].

Template patterns

Add seam allowances

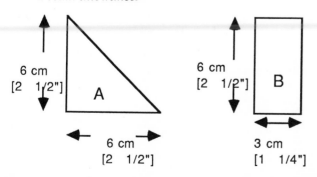

6 cm [2 1/2"]
6 cm [2 1/2"]

6 cm [2 1/2"]
3 cm [1 1/4"]

Cut out

• Varied prints
Template A cut 12
Template D cut 36
• White fabric
Template A cut 6
Template B cut 12
Template C cut 6
Template D cut 24
• Pale blue fabric
2 squares
6 large triangles
4 small triangles
• Blue fabric border strips 6 cm [2½"] wide plus seams.
• Binding strips, straight grain 5.2 cm [2"] wide.

Construction

• Piece basket blocks.
• Piece quilt by alternating plain blocks with basket blocks, setting blocks on the diagonal. Add borders.
• Mark quilting designs onto alternate blocks and borders. Flower and heart designs are appropriate.
• Assemble layers and quilt.
• Bind edges with strips making double binding.

The quilt and cushions in their favourite team's colours might appeal to big kids as well! (p 38)

Dresden Plate Quilt

Finished size

63 × 44 cm [25½ × 18″] not including binding.
3 × 2 blocks each 19 cm [7½″].

Requirements

• Assortment of scraps of pink and blue prints for plates.
• Cream fabric for background of blocks and centres 50 cm [½″ yd].
• Darker print for plates and first border 10 cm [4″].
• Fabric for second border and binding 30 cm [12″].
• Batting, 70 × 50 cm [28 × 20″].
• Backing fabric, 70 × 50 cm [28 × 20″].

Cut out

• Various prints, 72 segments.
• Cream fabric, 6 squares 19 cm [7½″] plus seams, 6 circle centres.

Template patterns

Do not add seam allowances

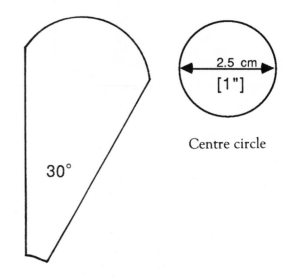

30°

2.5 cm
[1″]

Centre circle

• Darker print strips for first border 1 cm [½″] wide (plus seams).
• Second border, strips 2 cm [1″] wide plus seams.
• Binding strip (straight grain) 5.2 cm [2″] wide.

Construction

• Trace template onto cardboard and cut out (without seam allowances added). Mark and cut out segments.
• Assemble Dresden plates, stitching segments together along marked lines, but do not stitch across seam allowances at the outside of the plates (this is so that the seam allowances will turn back neatly and is a rare exception to the usual situation).
• Applique plates to background blocks. Add circles to centres, (using applique method for circles).
• Join blocks, 3 rows of 2 blocks each. Add borders.
• Mark quilting designs at block junctions.
• Assemble quilt layers. Outline quilt plates, blocks and borders. Quilt designs.
• Bind edges with strips (straight grain), to make double binding.

Train Quilt

For some little boys, it just has to be a train quilt.

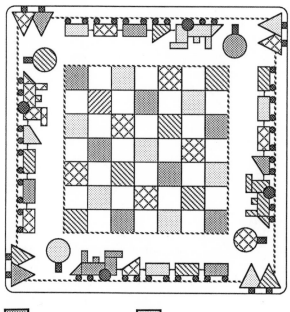

red   yellow

blue   green

Finished size

120 cm [48″] square, not including binding.

Requirements

• Blue, yellow and green fabric for squares, train and trees, 30 cm [12″] each.

• Red fabric for squares, train, trees and binding, 80 cm [1 yd].

• Background fabric for squares and borders, 1.5 m [1¾ yd].

• Navy fabric for wheels and tree trunks, 20 cm [8″].

• Batting, 130 × 130 cm [52 × 52″].

• Backing fabric, 1.8 m [2 yd]. Cut and join to make appropriate size.

• Navy ricrac for rails, 4.5 m [5 yd].

• Red ricrac for border around squares, 3 m [3¼ yd].

• Yellow ricrac for couplings, 1.6 m [2 yd].

• Very thin batting to line applique shapes, 50 cm [20″].

Template pattern

Add seam allowances

10cm
4 "

Cut out

• All squares to be cut 10 cm [4″] plus seam allowances. Cut 7 red, 7 yellow, 6 blue, 5 green and 24 from background fabric.

• Background fabric border strips 25 cm [10″] wide plus seam allowances.

• Red fabric strips (bias grain) for binding 8 cm [3″] wide.

• Train and tree shapes as indicated in diagram. Give these shapes 1 cm [⅜″] seam allowances.

Applique shapes

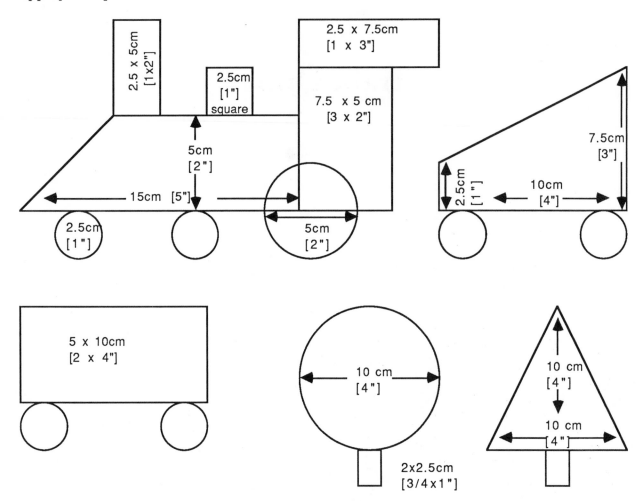

Construction

• Piece together centre squares, and add borders. Pencil mark a grid of intersecting lines across borders at 5 cm [2"] intervals, following lines from squares as guide for every second line.

• Assemble quilt layers and machine quilt along pencil lines and down seam lines between squares (this creates a grid of 10 cm [4"] over quilt centre and 5 cm [2"] through borders). Straight stitch close to edge of quilt and trim away excess batting and backing.

• Machine stitch red ricrac as border to centre squares, and navy ricrac for train line and yellow ricrac for couplings.

• Cut out applique shapes from firm cardboard. Use these as templates to mark applique pieces. Cut out the pieces, adding 1 cm [⅜"] seam allowances.

• Place fabric shapes right side down on ironing board. Place cardboard shape in centre, and steam press seam allowances firmly around cardboard shapes. Circles will need a row of running stitch to help the seam allowance pull smoothly round the shape. Remove cardboard.

• Use cardboard shape to cut out shapes from lightweight batting, cutting the shapes the exact size of the cardboard.

• Slip batting shapes behind fabric shapes, tucking seam allowances neatly around the batting at the edges, and pinning in place. Machine stitch around the outside of the shapes 2 mm [³⁄₁₆"] from their edges.

• Pin prepared applique shapes onto quilt and hand stitch in place.

• Bind edges of quilt with bias strips to make doubled binding. Curve binding around the corners.

Farm Life Quilt

This farm surely belongs to a member of the MacDonald family.

Finished size

160 × 144 cm [61 × 54"] not including binding.

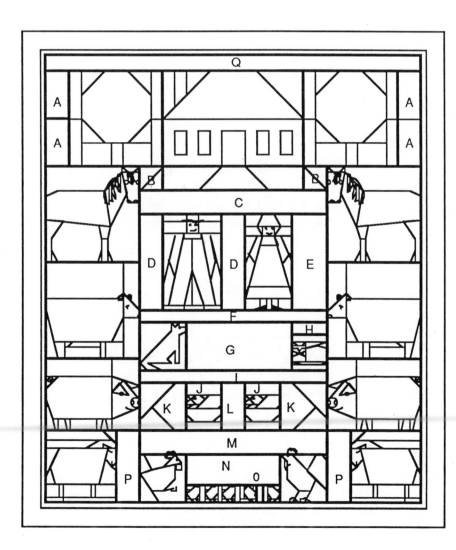

Background

a 16 × 8 cm [6 × 3"].
b 8 cm [3"] square cut on diagonal.
c 8 × 64 cm [3 × 24"].
d 32 × 8 cm [12 × 3"].
e 32 × 12 cm [12 × 4½"].
f 5 × 64 cm [1½ × 24"].
g 15 × 37 cm [6 × 14"].
h 3 × 12 cm [2 × 4"].
i 4 × 64 cm [1½ × 24"].
j 4 × 12 cm [2 × 4"].
k 16 × 16 cm [6 × 6"].
l 16 × 8 cm [6 × 4"].
m 8 × 64 cm [4 × 24"].
n 10 × 32 cm [4 × 12"].
o add extra 2 cm [2"] strip between two of the chicks.
p 24 × 8 cm [10 × 2"].
q 6 × 128 cm [2 × 48"].

Requirements

• Assortment of small pieces of printed fabric to make animals and farm, including green for trees, red for house roof, pale blue for sky, flower print for garden, grey for horse, brown for cow, pink for pig, beige for sheep, blue for duck pond, deep orange for fowls, yellow for chicks, black and white for dog, orange for cat.

Green print fabric for background, 2 m [2¼ yd].

• White fabric for inside border, house and ducks, 50 cm [½ yd].

• Print fabric for outside border, 60 cm [¾ yd].

• Batting 155 × 170 cm [58 × 65″].

• Backing fabric 3 m [3¼ yd].

• Fabric for binding 50 cm [½ yd].

• Assortment of embroidery threads for animal features.

Cut out

• Blocks according to instructions following.

• Background areas as given in key to quilt plan (plus seams).

• White inside border strips 2 cm [¾″] wide (plus seams).

• Print outside border strips 6 cm [2¼″] wide (plus seams).

• Strips (straight grain) for binding 8 cm [3″] wide.

Construction

• Construct pictorial farm blocks in the sizes indicated. Applique and embroider details. Note that many of the features on the blocks are three dimensional, e.g. ears on pig and sheep, hat on farmer, etc.

• Cut out templates for spaces between blocks, as indicated in quilt plan. Mark and cut out these from background fabric, sky, or duck pond fabric as appropriate. Join pieces to farm blocks to make the squares and rectangles marked by bold lines in the quilt plan.

• Join the squares and rectangles to form the quilt top. First join the pieces into four sections (1 house and trees; 2 animals on left; 3 centre section of quilt; 4 animals on right). Then join the sections together.

• Add borders, joining strips to make the lengths required. Mark clamshell quilting pattern on background.

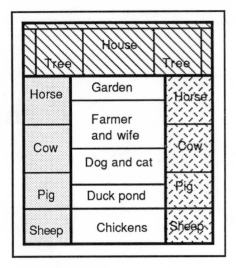

Construct quilt in 4 sections, then join sections together.

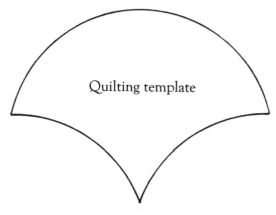

Quilting template

• Assemble quilt top, batting and backing and prepare for quilting. Quilt around motifs and quilt clamshell pattern into background.

• Bind edges of quilt with strips making a doubled binding.

House

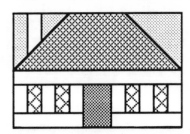

Size for quilt
32 × 48 cm [12 × 18″]
4 × 6 squares each 8 cm [3″]

Colour

White house and chimney
6, 7, 9, 11, 14, 16, 18
Terracotta roof **4**
Red door **13**
Yellow print windows **8, 10, 15, 17**
Background (sky) **1, 3, 5**

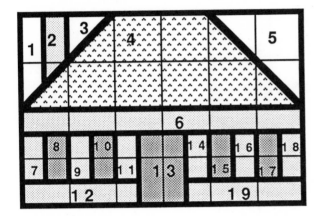

Tree and Edge

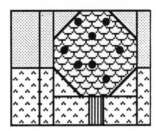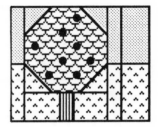

Size for quilt

32 cm [12″] square
4 × 4 squares each 8 cm [3″]

Colour

Brown trunk **2**
Green print foliage **4**
Green ground **1, 3, 5, 6, 10, 12**
Background (sky) **7, 8, 9, 11**

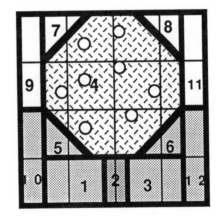

Piecing order

1 **1 + 2 + 3**
2 **(1–3) + 4 + 5**
3 **7 + 8 + 9 + 10 + 11**
4 **(7–11) + 12**
5 **14 + 15 + 16 + 17 + 18**
6 **(14–18) + 19**
7 **(7–12) + 13 + (14–19)**
8 **(1–5) + 6 + (7–19)**

Piecing order

1 **1 + 2 + 3**
2 **4 + 5 + 6 + 7 + 8**
3 **(1–3) + (4–8)**
4 **9 + 10**
5 **11 + 12**
6 **(1–8) + (9–10) + (11–12)**
Applique circles for apples.

Garden

Cut out

Flowers **1, 3**
Path **2**

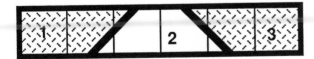

Piecing order

1 **1 + 2 + 3**

Horse

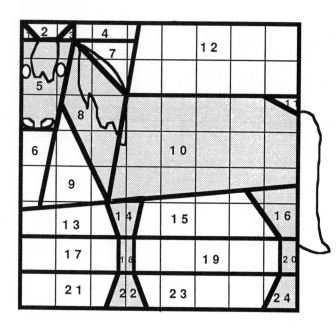

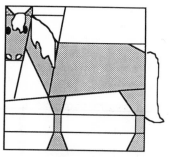

Size for quilt

32 cm [12″] square
8 × 8 squares each 4 cm [1½″]

Colour

Grey horse **1, 3, 5, 8, 10, 14, 16, 18, 20, 22, 24.**
Background **2, 4, 6, 7, 9, 11, 12, 13, 15, 17, 19, 21, 23.**

Piecing order

1   **1 + 2 + 3 + 4**
2   **5 + 6**
3   **7 + 8 + 9**
4   **(5−6) + (7−9)**
5   **(1−4) + (5−9)**
6   **10 + 11**
7   **(10−11) + 12**
8   **(1−9) + (10−12)**
9   **13 + 14 + 15 + 16**
10   **17 + 18 + 19 + 20**
11   **21 + 22 + 23 + 24**
12   **(1−12) + (13−16) + (17−20) + (21−24)**
Applique mane and tail. Embroider eyes and nostrils.

For other projects the block may be made in a different size e.g. 24 cm [10″] square. Each square, 3 cm [1¼″].

Cow

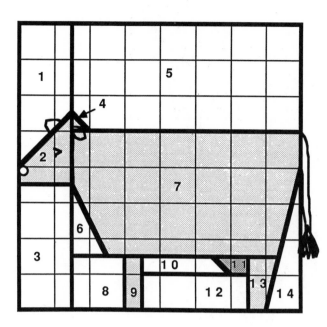

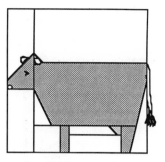

Size for quilt

32 cm [12"] square
8 × 8 squares each 4 cm [1½"]

Colour

Brown cow **2, 4, 7, 9, 13**, ears, tail.
Pink udder **11**.
Background **1, 3, 5, 6, 8, 10, 12, 14**.

Piecing order

Cut out shape for cows right ear, and applique in place onto piece 1.

1. **1 + 2 + 3**
2. **4 + 5**
3. **6 + 7**
4. **10 + 11**
5. **(10–11) + 12**
6. **8 + 9 + (10–12) + 13**
7. **(4–5) + (6–7) + (8–13)**
8. **(4–13) + 14**

Cut out two shapes for cows left ear, pin right sides together and machine stitch. Trim seams, turn right side out, and press. Pin in place onto piece **4**. (This makes a 3D ear.)

9. **(1–3) + (4–17)**

Embroider tail, eye and nostril. If preferred, tail can be made from rouleau, with a tassel at the end.

> For other projects the block may be made in a different size e.g. 24 cm [10"] square. Each square, 3 cm [1¼"].

Sheep

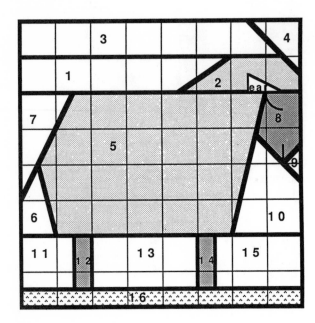

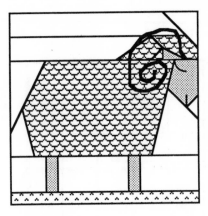

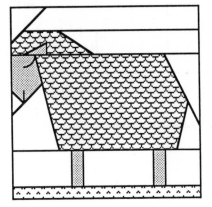

Size for quilt

24 cm [10″] square
8 × 8 squares each 3 cm [1¼″]

Colour

Beige sheep body **2, 5**.
Light brown face and legs **8, 12, 14**.
Grass or background **16**.
Background **1, 3, 4, 6, 7, 9, 10, 11, 13, 15**.

Piecing order

1 **1 + 2**
2 **(1–2) + 3**
3 **(1–3) + 4**
4 **5 + 6**
5 **(5–6) + 7**
6 **8 + 9**
7 **(8–9) + 10**

8 **(5–7) + (8–10)**
9 **11 + 12 + 13 + 14 + 15**

Construct ear. Cut two ear shapes. Stitch together, and turn right side out. Pin in place on piece 2 (this makes a 3D ear).

10 **(1–4) + (5–9) + (11–15) + 16**

Note that the ear will be sewn in place in the seam between section (**1–4**) and (**5–9**).

Embroider eye and mouth. Horns can be embroidered to make a ram.

> For other projects the block may be made in a different size e.g.
> 28 cm [8″] square. Each square, 2.5 cm [1″].
> 32 cm [12″] square. Each square, 4 cm [1½″].

Pig

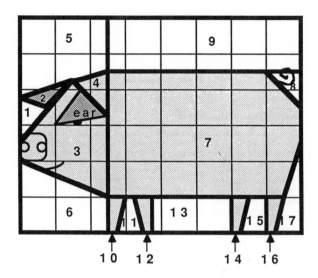

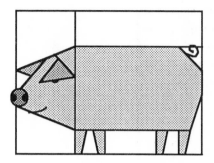

Size for quilt

24 × 32 cm [9 × 12″]
6 × 8 squares each 4 cm [1½″]

Colour

Deep pink features **2**, 3D ear, nose.
Pink pig **3, 4, 7, 10, 12, 14, 16**.
Background **1, 5, 6, 8, 9, 11, 13, 15, 17**.

Piecing order

  1   **1 + 2**
Make pigs left ear. Cut two ear shapes, stitch together, turn right side out. Pin in place on piece 3. (This makes a 3D ear.)
  2   **3 + 4**
  3   **(1–2) + (3–4)**
  4   **(1–4) + 5**
  5   **(1–5) + 6**
  6   **7 + 8**
  7   **(7–8) + 9**
  8   **10 + 11 + 12 + 13 + 14 + 15 + 16**
  9   **(7–9) + (10–16)**
10   **(7–16) + 17**
11   **(1–6) + (7–17)**
Applique nose. Embroider eye, mouth and nostrils.
Make tail from bias rouleau.

> *For other projects the block may be made in a different size e.g. 24 cm [10″] square. Each square, 3 cm [1¼″].*

Farmer

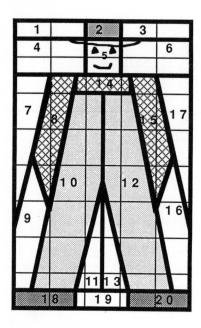

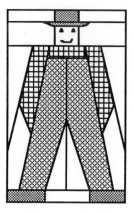

Finished size

32 × 20 cm [12 × 7½″]
8 × 5 squares each 4 cm [1½″]

Colour

Light brown hat **2** and hat brim.
Pink face **5**.
Red check shirt **8, 14, 15**.
Blue overalls **10, 12**.
Brown boots **18, 20**.
Background **1, 3, 4, 6, 7, 9, 11, 13, 16, 17, 19**.

Piecing order

 1 **1 + 2 + 3**

Hat brim; cut two shallow semicircles from hat fabric. Right sides together, stitch around outside edge. Turn right side out and press. Pin onto piece 2 (this makes a 3D brim).

 2 **4 + 5 + 6**
 3 **8 + 9**
 4 **7 + (8–9)**
 5 **10 + 11**
 6 **12 + 13**
 7 **(10–11) + (12–13)**
 8 **(10–13) + 14**
 9 **15 + 16**
10 **(15–16) + 17**
11 **(7–9) + (10–14) + (15–17)**
12 **18 + 19 + 20**
13 **(1–3) + (4–6) + (7–17) + (18–20)**

Note that the hat brim will be sewn in when sections **(1–3)** and **(4–6)** are sewn together. Embroider face.

Wife

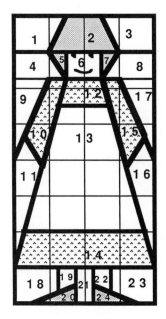 

Finished size

32 × 16 cm [12 × 6″]
8 × 4 squares each 4 cm [1½″]

Colour

Brown hair 2, 5, 7.
Pink face and legs 6, 19, 22.
Rose dress 10, 12, 14, 15.
White apron 13.
Brown shoes 20, 24.
Background 1, 3, 4, 8, 9, 11, 16, 17, 18, 21, 23.

Piecing order

1 1 + 2 + 3
2 4 + 5
3 7 + 8
4 (4–5) + 6 + (7–8)
5 10 + 11
6 9 + (10–11)
7 12 + 13 + 14
8 15 + 16
9 (15–16) + 17
10 (9–11) + (12–14) + (15–17)
11 18 + 19

12 (18–19) + 20
13 22 + 23
14 (22–23) + 24
15 (18–20) + 21 + (22–24)
16 (1–3) + (4–8) + (9–17) + (18–24)
Embroider face.

Duck

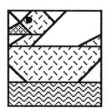 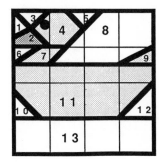

Size for quilt

12 cm [4″] square
4 × 4 squares each 3 cm [1″]

Colour

Yellow bill 2.
White duck 4, 7, 9, 11.
Water 13.
Background 1, 3, 5, 6, 8, 10, 12.

Piecing order

1 1 + 2
2 3 + 4 + 5
3 (1–2) + (3–5)
4 6 + 7
5 (1–5) + (6–7)
6 8 + 9
7 (1–7) + (8–9)
8 10 + 11 + 12
9 (1–9) + (10–12) + 13
Embroider eye.

Rooster

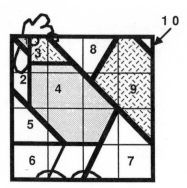

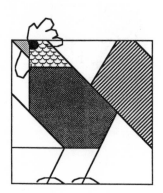

Size for quilt

16 cm [6"] square
4 × 4 squares each 4 cm [1½"]

Colour

Deep orange print head and tail 9, 3.
Deep orange body 4.
Yellow beak 1.
Background 2, 5, 6, 7, 8, 10.

Piecing order

1 1 + 2
2 3 + 4
3 (1–2) + (3–4)
4 (1–4) + 5
5 (1–5) + 6
6 (1–6) + 7
7 8 + 9
8 (8–9) + 10
9 (1–7) + (8–10)
Applique red comb and wattle.
Embroider eye, legs and feet.

Hen

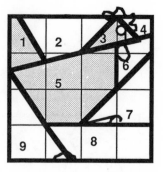

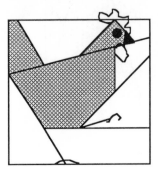

Size as for rooster

Colour

Deep orange 1, 3, 5.
Background 2, 4, 6, 7, 8, 9.

Piecing order

Stitch a scrap of fabric over the tip of piece 3 to
make a beak.
1 1 + 2 + 3 + 4
2 5 + 6
3 (5–6) + 7
4 (5–7) + 8
5 (5–8) + 9
6 (1–4) + (5–9).
Applique red comb and wattle.
Embroider eye, legs and feet.

*For other projects the block may be made in a
different size e.g. 20 cm [8"] square. Each square,
5 cm [2"].*

Chick

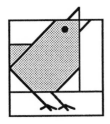

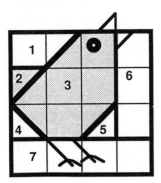

Size for quilt

6 cm [2″] square
4 × 4 squares each 1.5 cm [½″]

Colour

Yellow chick **2**, **3**.
Background **1**, **4**, **5**, **6**, **7**.

Piecing order

1 **1 + 2**
2 **3 + 4 + 5**
3 **(1–2) + (3–5)**
4 **(1–5) + 6**
5 **(1–6) + 7**
Embroider beak, eye and legs.

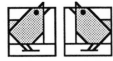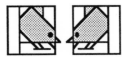

Rotate block to make chicks peck.

*For other projects the block may be made in a
different size e.g. 8 cm [3″] square. Each square,
2 cm [¾″].*

Dog

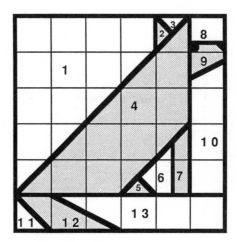

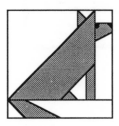

Size for quilt

15 cm [6″] square
6 × 6 squares each 2.5 cm [1″]

Colour

Black and white print dog **2**, **4**, **5**, **7**, **9**, **12**.
Background **1**, **3**, **6**, **8**, **10**, **11**, **13**.

Piecing order

1 **1 + 2 + 3**
2 **5 + 6 + 7**
3 **4 + (5–7)**
4 **(1–3) + (4–7)**
5 **8 + 9 + 10**
6 **(1–7) + (8–10)**
7 **11 + 12 + 13**
8 **(1–10) + (11–13)**
Embroider eye and nose.

*For other projects the block may be made in a
different size e.g. 24 cm [9″] square. Each square,
4 cm [1½″].*

Cat

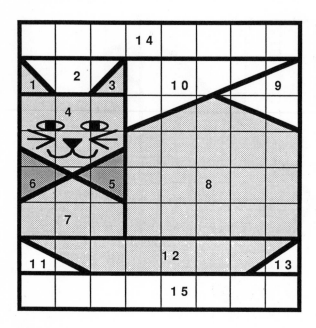

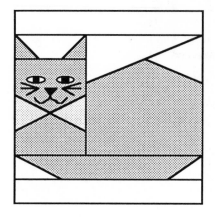

Size for quilt

12 cm [4″] square
8 × 8 squares each 1.5 cm [½″]

Colour

Orange cat **1, 3, 4, 7, 8, 12.**
White bow **5, 6.**
Background **2, 9, 11, 13, 14, 15.**

Piecing order

1 **1 + 2 + 3**
2 **4 + 5**
3 **6 + 7**

4 **(1–3) + (4–5) + (6–7)**
5 **8 + 9**
6 **(8–9) + 10**
7 **(1–7) + (8–10)**
8 **11 + 12 + 13**
9 **(1–10) + (11–13) + 14 + 15**
Embroider eye, nose, mouth and whiskers.

> *For other projects the block may be made in a*
> *different size e.g.*
> *12 cm [5″] square. Each square, 1.5 cm [⅝″].*
> *16 cm [6″] square. Each square, 2 cm [¾″].*
> *20 cm [8″] square. Each square, 2.5 cm [1″].*
> *24 cm [10″] square. Each square, 3 cm [1¼″].*
> *32 cm [12″] square. Each square, 4 cm [1½″].*

Farm Life quilt: this utterly charming quilt will be everybody's favourite (p 47)

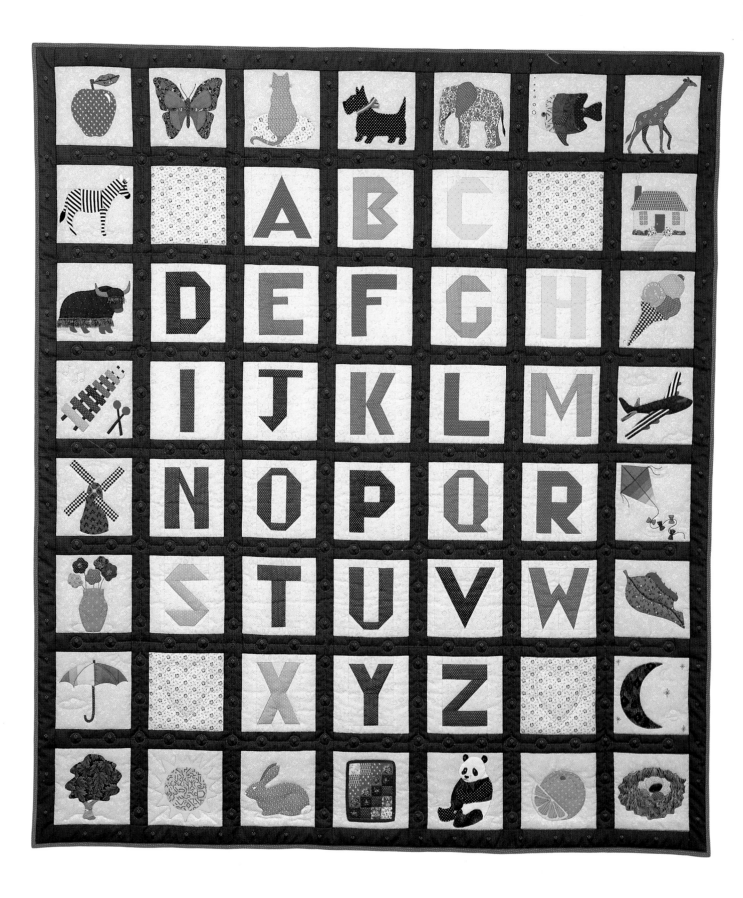

Alphabet quilt: alphabets have a special place in patchwork for children. This superb
quilt has an appliqued motif representing each letter. Made by Trudy Brodie

Alphabet Quilt

Alphabet quilts will always have a special place amongst quilts for children. This one designed itself when I discovered that if the alphabet was put into 6 rows of 5 blocks (leaving 4 plain blocks in each corner), then there were exactly 26 blocks around the outside.

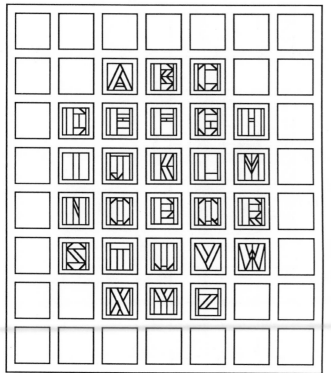

Finished size

164 × 144 cm [61½ × 54″].

Requirements

• Dark green print fabric for sashing, 2.5 m [2¾ yd].

• Light green and cream print fabric for background of pieced blocks, 90 cm [1 yd]. If desired, the plain blocks can be made from a different print. 20 cm [8″] fabric will be needed.

• Light green and cream print for background of applique blocks, 90 cm [1 yd].

• Rainbow colours, yellow, orange, red, bluish red, purple, blue, green, yellowgreen, for pieced alphabet and applique. 20 cm [8″] each.

• Assortment of bright coloured scraps for applique

• Red print for binding, 50 cm [20″].

• Batting, 180 × 160 cm [66 × 58″].

• Backing fabric, 3.1 m [3¼ yd].

Construction

• Piece alphabet blocks, 12 cm [5″] square. Add strips 2 cm [½″] around each block to make them 16 cm [6″] square not including seam allowances.

• Cut background blocks for applique. Cut 26 blocks each 16 cm [6″] square (plus seams). Applique motifs to blocks and embroider details.

• Cut strips for sashing 4 cm [1½″] wide plus seams. Join sashing to blocks to make quilt top.

• Assemble quilt layers and outline quilt sashing and motifs.

• Bind edges of quilt with strips (bias), cut 6 cm [2½″] to make double binding.

Alphabet designs

Block size 12 cm [5″] square
8 × 8 squares, each square 1.5 cm [⅝″]
Note that only some letters take up the whole square. Most letters take up ¾ of the square, and will have strips each side to make up the square. Only one template need be made of this shape, except for the letter I which has wider strips.

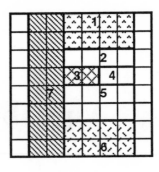

1 1 + 2
2 3 + 4
3 (1–2) + (3–4) + 5 + 6
4 (1–6) + 7

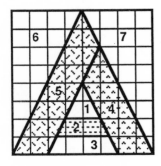

1 1 + 2 + 3
2 (1–3) + 4
3 (1–4) + 5
4 (1–5) + 6
5 (1–6) + 7

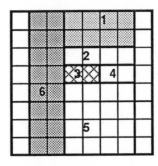

1 1 + 2
2 3 + 4
3 (1–2) + (3–4) + 5
4 (1–5) + 6

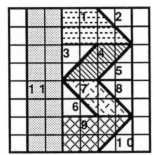

1 1 + 2
2 3 + 4 + 5
3 6 + 7 + 8
4 9 + 10
5 (1–2) + (3–5) + (6–8) + (9–10)
6 (1–10) + 11

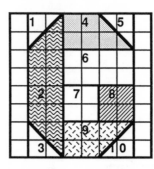

1 1 + 2 + 3
2 4 + 5
3 7 + 8
4 9 + 10
5 (4–5) + 6 + (7–8) + (9–10)
6 (1–3) + (4–10)

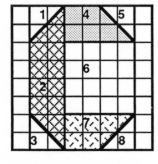

1 1 + 2 + 3
2 4 + 5
3 7 + 8
4 (4–5) + 6 + (7–8)
5 (1–3) + (4–8)

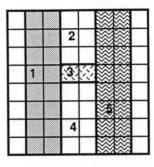

1 2 + 3 + 4
2 1 + (2–4) + 5

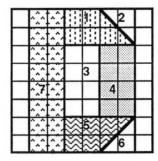

1 1 + 2
2 3 + 4
3 5 + 6
4 (1–2) + (3–4) + (5–6)
5 (1–6) + 7

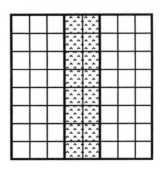

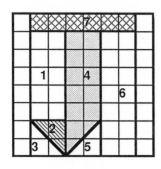

1   **1 + 2 + 3**
2   **4 + 5**
3   **(1−3) + (4−5) + 6**
4   **(1−6) + 7**

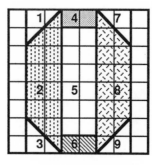

1   **1 + 2 + 3**
2   **4 + 5 + 6**
3   **7 + 8 + 9**
4   **(1−3) + (4−6) +**
    (7−9)

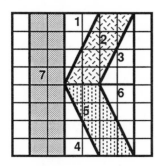

1   **1 + 2 + 3**
2   **4 + 5 + 6**
3   **(1−3) + (4−6)**
4   **(1−6) + 7**

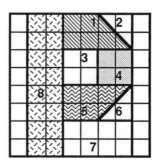

1   **1 + 2**
2   **3 + 4**
3   **5 + 6**
4   **(1−2) + (3−4) +**
    (5−6) + 7
5   **(1−7) + 8**

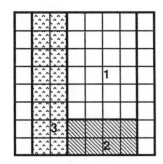

1   **1 + 2**
2   **(1−2) + 3**

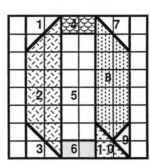

1   **1 + 2 + 3**
2   **4 + 5 + 6**
3   **7 + 8 + 9**
4   **(7−9) + 10**
5   **(1−3) + (4−6) +**
    (7−10)

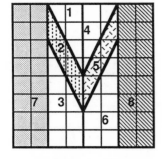

1   **1 + 2 + 3**
2   **4 + 5 + 6**
3   **(1−3) + (4−6)**
4   **(1−6) + 7 + 8**

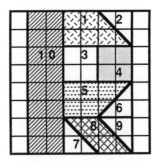
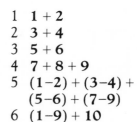

1   **1 + 2**
2   **3 + 4**
3   **5 + 6**
4   **7 + 8 + 9**
5   **(1−2) + (3−4) +**
    (5−6) + (7−9)
6   **(1−9) + 10**

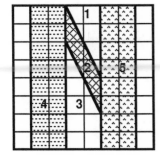

1   **1 + 2 + 3**
2   **(1−3) + 4 + 5**

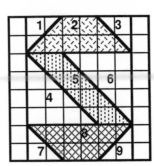

1   **1 + 2 + 3**
2   **4 + 5 + 6**
3   **7 + 8 + 9**
4   **(1−3) + (4−6) +**
    (7−9)

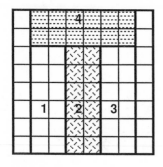

1   **1 + 2 + 3**
2   **(1–3) + 4**

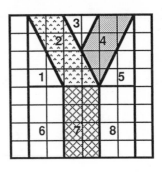

1   **1 + 2**
2   **3 + 4 + 5**
3   **(1–2) + (3–5)**
4   **6 + 7 + 8**
5   **(1–5) + (6–8)**

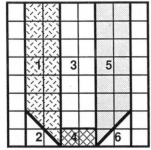

1   **1 + 2**
2   **3 + 4**
3   **5 + 6**
4   **(1–2) + (3–4) +**
     (5–6)

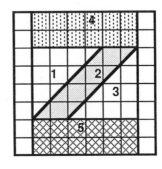

1   **1 + 2 + 3**
2   **(1–3) + 4 + 5**

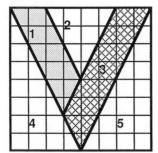

1   **1 + 2**
2   **(1–2) + 3**
3   **(1–3) + 4**
4   **(1–4) + 5**

Making the letters into words

The letters can be used to make words and names. Because the letters take up differing amounts of a square, they will need to be spaced appropriately for their size. For instance, the space around the letter I should be made to be the same as the majority of other letters. If two of the larger letters (A, M, V, W) are put next to each other, put a space between them.

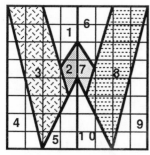

1   **1 + 2**
2   **(1–2) + 3 + 4**
3   **(1–4) + 5**
4   **6 + 7**
5   **(6–7) + 8 + 9**
6   **(6–9) + 10**
7   **(1–5) + (6–10)**

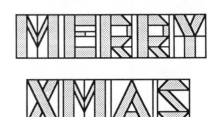

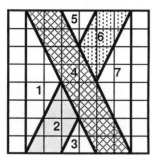

1   **1 + 2 + 3**
2   **(1–3) + 4**
3   **5 + 6 + 7**
4   **(1–4) + (5–7)**

Alphabet applique patterns

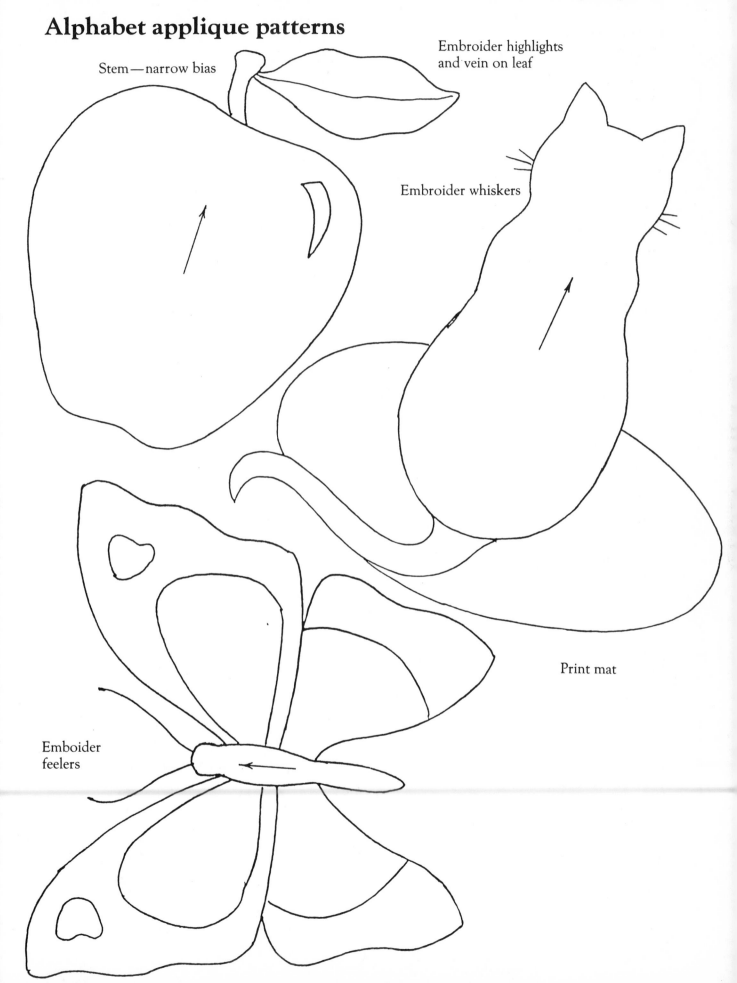

Stem—narrow bias

Embroider highlights
and vein on leaf

Embroider whiskers

Print mat

Emboider
feelers

Embroider eye
and nose

Embroider bubbles
(outline only)

Tartan ribbon

Embroider tusk,
eye and tail

Embroider window
divisions and door
handle

Embroider highlight
on cherry

Use print to suggest
flower beds and bushes
by door

Embroider eye,
mane, tail

Check fabric for cone

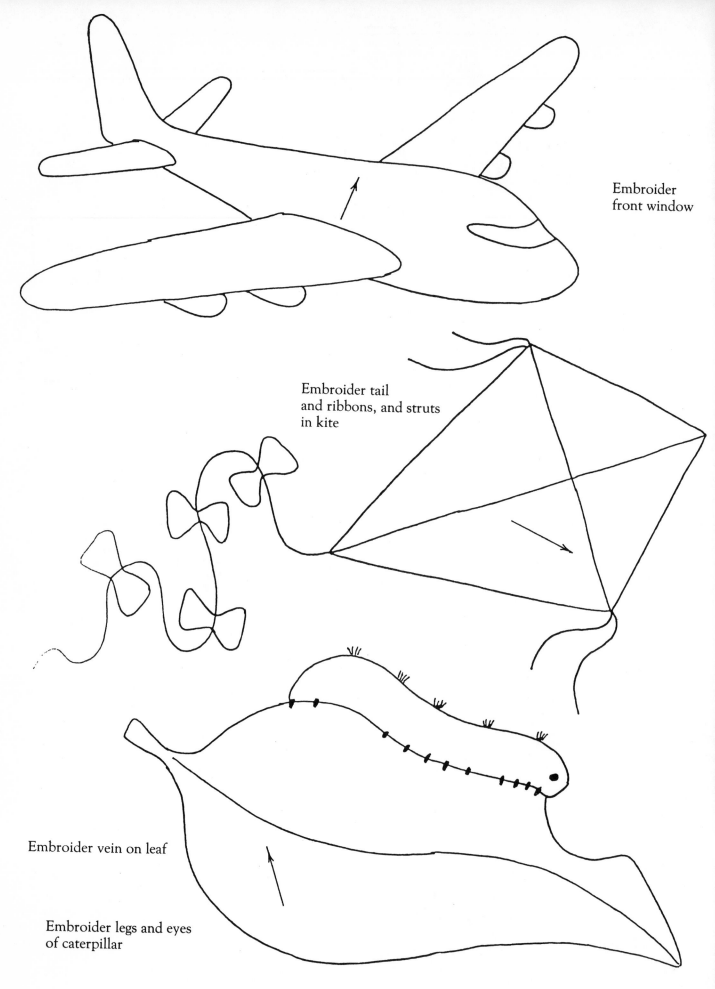

Embroider
front window

Embroider tail
and ribbons, and struts
in kite

Embroider vein on leaf

Embroider legs and eyes
of caterpillar

Embroider stars

Applique in layers; first inside of nest,
then eggs and lastly outside

Embroider dark spot

Embroider nose, mouth, eyes and bamboo

Right arm and upper part of body can be one piece

Place small neck piece behind head and upper body

Piece 2 cm [⅞″] squares together, then bind with narrow bias, and applique in place. Quilting along seam lines will make the squares puff up

Use print for foliage

Embroider eye and nose

Rouleau for handle and tip

Embroider spines

Embroider arms

Check fabric for sails

Embroider stems
French knots for flower centres

70

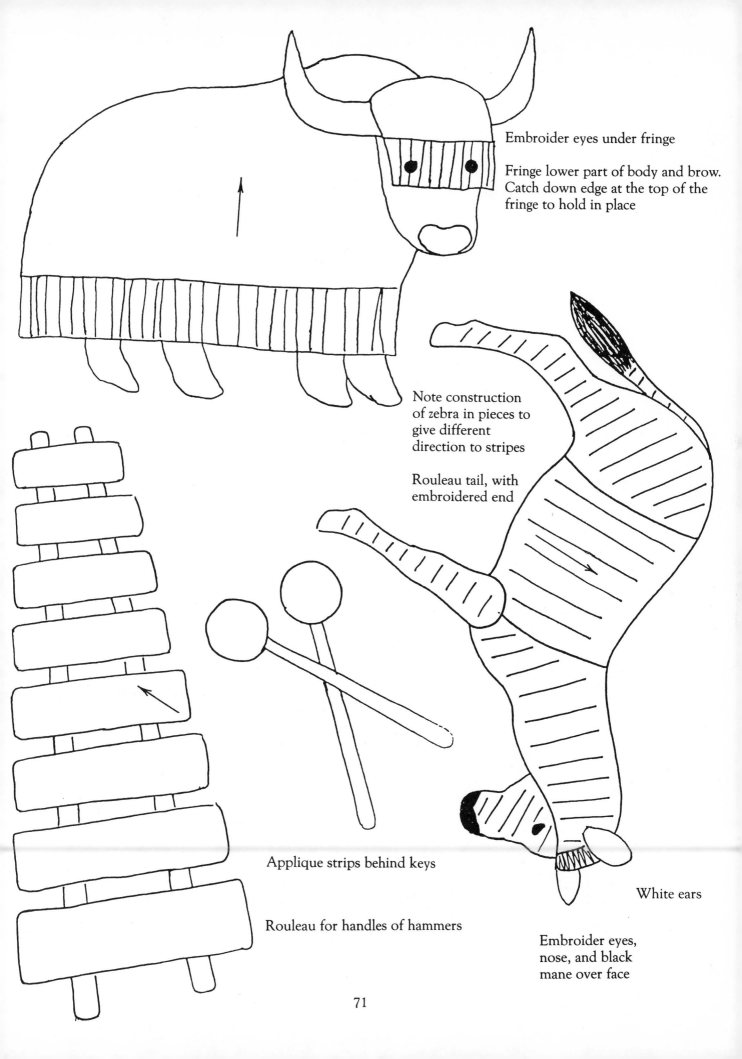

Embroider eyes under fringe

Fringe lower part of body and brow.
Catch down edge at the top of the
fringe to hold in place

Note construction
of zebra in pieces to
give different
direction to stripes

Rouleau tail, with
embroidered end

Applique strips behind keys

Rouleau for handles of hammers

White ears

Embroider eyes,
nose, and black
mane over face

Dinosaur continental quilt cover

There is a phase many children go through when dinosaurs are their favourite animals. Make this dinosaur cover for a continental quilt.

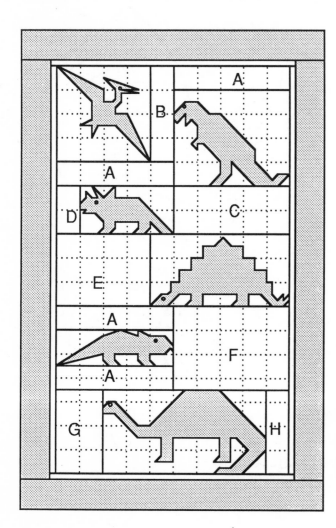

Finished size

200 × 130 cm [80 × 52″].

Requirements

• Jungle print for background 2.5 m [2¾ yd].
• Red for first border 30 cm [12″].
• Navy for dinosaurs, outside border, and back of quilt cover 5 m [5½ yd].
• Navy bias binding 2.6 m [3 yd].
• 4 snap fasteners.

Construction

• Piece the animal blocks
• Construct the centre of the cover top by adding rectangles (as shown in diagram).
• Add border of red, cut strips 2.5 cm [1″] wide (plus seams).
• Add border of navy, cut strips 12.5 cm [5″] wide (plus seams).

A - 10 x 50 cm [4 x 20"]	E - 30 x 40 cm [12 x 16"]
B - 40 x 10cm [16 x 4"]	F - 35 x 50 cm [14 x 20"]
C - 20 x 50 cm [8 x 20"]	G - 35 x 20 cm [14 x 8"]
D - 20 x 10 cm [8 x 4"]	H - 35 x 10 cm [14 x 4"]

• Make back of cover from navy fabric, 200 × 130 cm [80 × 52″] plus seam allowances.

• Face bottom edge of both top and back with navy bias binding.

• With right sides together, stitch top to back, leaving a large space at the bottom for the opening. Turn right side out.

• Apply snaps to opening.

Pteranodon

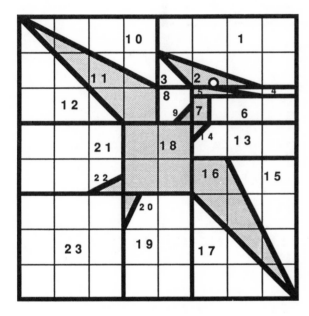

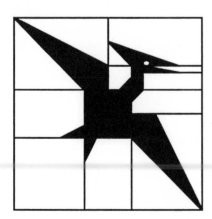

Size for quilt cover

40 × 40 cm [16 × 16″]
8 × 8 squares each 5 cm [2″]

Colour

Pteranodon 2, 5, 7, 9, 11, 14. 16, 18, 20, 22.
Background 1, 3, 4, 6, 8, 10, 12, 13, 15, 17, 19, 21, 23.

Piecing order

```
 1   1 + 2 + 3
 2   4 + 5
 3   6 + 7
 4   (4–5) + (6–7)
 5   8 + 9
 6   (4–7) + (8–9)
 7   (1–3) + (4–9)
 8   10 + 11 + 12
 9   (1–9) + (10–12)
10   13 + 14
11   15 + 16 + 17
12   (13–14) + (15–17)
13   19 + 20
14   18 + (19–20)
15   21 + 22
16   (21–22) + 23
17   (13–17) + (18–20) + (21–23)
18   (1–12) + (13–23)
```
Applique eye.

Brontosaurus

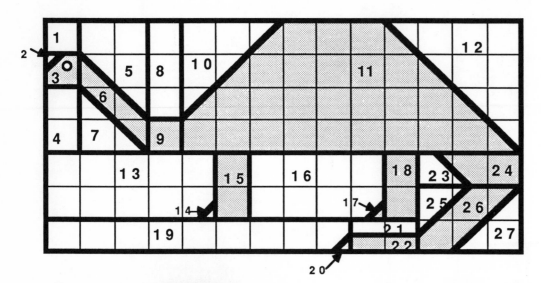

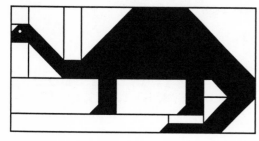

Size for quilt cover

35 × 70 cm [14 × 28″]
7 × 14 squares each 5 cm [2″]

Colour

Brontosaurus 3, 6, 9, 11, 14, 15, 17, 18, 20, 22,
24, 26.
Background 1, 2, 4, 5, 7, 8, 10, 12, 13, 16, 19,
21, 23, 25, 27.

Piecing order

1   2 + 3
2   1 + (2–3) + 4
3   5 + 6 + 7
4   8 + 9
5   10 + 11 + 12
6   (1–4) + (5–7) + (8–9) + (10–12)
7   13 + 14
8   15 + 16 + 17
9   (13–14) + (15–17) + 18
10 19 + 20
11 21 + 22
12 (19–20) + (21–22)
13 (13–18) + (19–22)
14 23 + 24
15 25 + 26 + 27
16 (23–24) + (25–27)
17 (13–22) + (23–27)
18 (1–12) + (13–27)
Applique eye.

Dinosaur continental quilt cover: all children who like dinosaurs will be fascinated
by these prehistoric animals enjoying their vivid jungle (p 72). Made by
Christa Roksandic

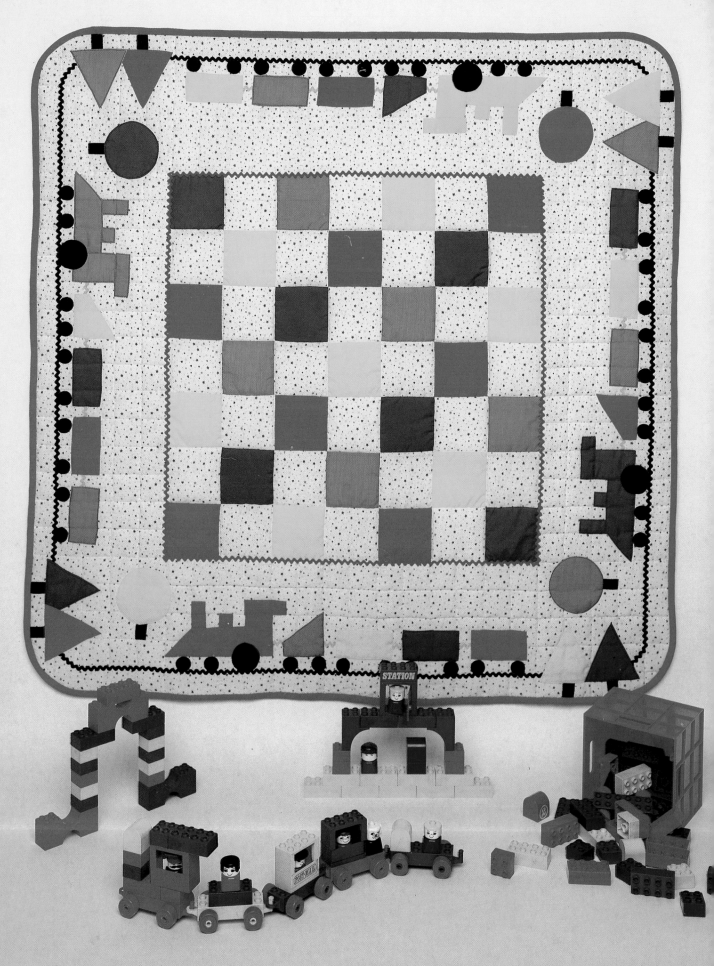

These terrific trains are bound for the land of nod. This cot quilt combines
patchwork and applique (p 45)

Triceratops

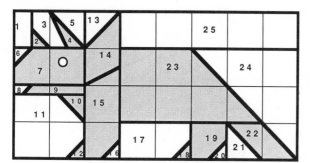

Size for quilt cover

20 × 40 cm [8 × 16″]
4 × 8 squares each 5 cm [2″]

Colour

Triceratops 2, 4, 7, 9, 10, 12, 14, 15, 18, 19, 22, 23.
Background 1, 3, 5, 6, 8, 11, 13, 16, 17, 20, 21, 24, 25.

Piecing order

1   2 + 3 + 4 + 5
2   1 + (2–5)
3   6 + 7
4   8 + 9
5   10 + 11 + 12
6   (1–5) + (6–7) + (8–9) + (10–12)
7   13 + 14 + 15 + 16
8   17 + 18
9   19 + 20
10   (17–18) + (19–20) + 21 + 22
11   (17–22) + 23
12   (17–23) + 24
13   (17–24) + 25
14   (1–12) + (13–16) + (17–25)
Applique eye.

Protoceratops

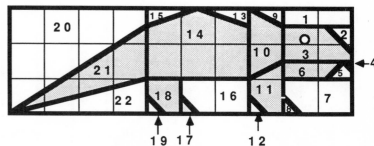

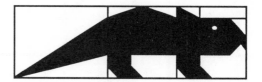

Size for quilt cover

15 × 50 cm [6 × 20″]
3 × 10 squares each 5 cm [2″]

Colour

Protoceratops 3, 4, 6, 8, 10, 11, 14, 17, 18, 21.
Background 1, 2, 5, 7, 9, 12, 13, 15, 16, 19, 20, 22.

Piecing order

1   2 + 3
2   4 + 5
3   (4–5) + 6
4   7 + 8
5   1 + (2–3) + (4–6) + (7–8)
6   9 + 10 + 11 + 12
7   13 + 14 + 15
8   16 + 17
9   18 + 19
10   (16–17) + (18–19)
11   (13–15) + (16–19)
12   20 + 21 + 22
13   (1–8) + (9–12) + (13–19) + (20–22)
Applique eye.

Tyrannosaurus

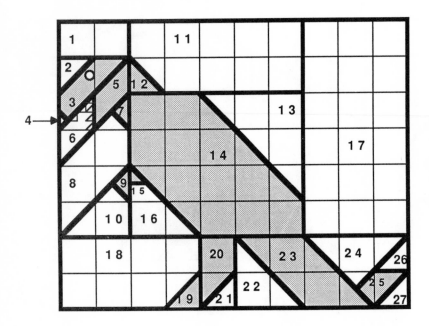

Size for quilt cover

40 × 50 cm [16 × 20″]
8 × 10 squares each 5 cm [2″]

Colour

Tyrannosaurus 3, 5, 7, 9, 12, 14, 15, 19, 20, 23, 25.
Background 1, 2, 4, 6, 8, 10, 11, 13, 16, 17, 18, 21, 22, 24, 26, 27.

Piecing order

1   3 + 4
2   2 + (3–4)
3   5 + 6
4   7 + 8
5   9 + 10
6   1 + (2–4) + (5–6) + (7–8) + (9–10)
7   11 + 12
8   15 + 16
9   13 + 14 + (15–16)
10   (11–12) + (13–16)
11   (1–10) + (11–16) + 17
12   18 + 19
13   20 + 21
14   22 + 23
15   25 + 26
16   24 + (25–26) + 27
17   (18–19) + (20–21) + (22–23) + (24–27)
18   (1–17) + (18–27)

Applique eye and embroider teeth if desired.

Stegosaurus

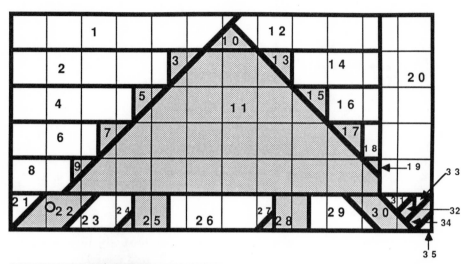

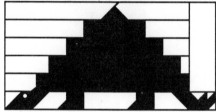

Size for quilt cover

30 × 60 cm [12 × 24″]
6 × 12 squares each 5 cm [2″]

Colour

Stegosaurus **3, 5, 7, 9, 10, 11, 13, 15, 17, 19, 22, 24, 25, 27, 28, 30, 32, 34.**
Background **1, 2, 4, 6, 8, 12, 14, 16, 18, 20, 21, 23, 26, 29, 31, 33, 35.**

Piecing order

  1 **2 + 3**
  2 **4 + 5**
  3 **6 + 7**
  4 **8 + 9**
  5 **1 + (2−3) + (4−5) + (6−7) + (8−9)**
  6 **10 + 11**
  7 **13 + 14**
  8 **15 + 16**
  9 **17 + 18**
10 **12 + (13−14) + (15−16) + (17−18) + 19**
11 **(10−11) + (12−19)**
12 **(1−9) + (10−19)**
13 **(1−19) + 20**
14 **21 + 22 + 23 + 24**
15 **25 + 26 + 27**
16 **28 + 29 + 30**
17 **32 + 33**
18 **31 + (32−33) + 34 + 35**
19 **(21−24) + (25−27) + (28−30) + (31−35)**
20 **(1−20) + (21−35)**
Applique eye.

Elephant Quilt

A herd of pastel coloured elephants makes a delightful quilt for baby.

Finished size

120 cm [45"] square not including binding.

Requirements

• Gingham in pink, lavender, lemon and aqua for elephants, squares and triangles 40 cm [½ yd] each.

• White and pastel print fabric for background of elephants and triangles, 1 m [1¼ yd].

• Print fabric for sashing, binding 1.3 m [1½ yd].

• Batting, 145 × 145 cm [54 × 54"].

• Backing fabric, 2 m [2¼ yd].

• Stranded embroidery thread to match gingham.

Template shapes

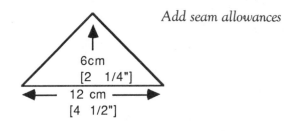

Add seam allowances

6cm
[2 1/4"]

12 cm
[4 1/2"]

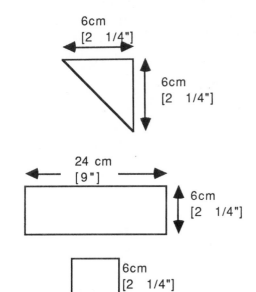

6cm
[2 1/4"]

6cm
[2 1/4"]

24 cm
[9"]

6cm
[2 1/4"]

6cm
[2 1/4"]
square

Cut out

• 9 elephant blocks, 6 facing left, 3 facing right.

• Rectangles and squares for sashing, using template shapes for sizes

• For border, cut 72 triangles (18 of each gingham) and 144 smaller triangles of background fabric.

Construction

• Piece elephant blocks. Make ears with gingham squares on the bias, but cut the rest of the elephant with the straight grain as usual. Reverse the templates to make the elephants going the opposite way. Embroider details.

• Cut rectangles and squares for sashing. Assemble centre section of quilt. Cut out triangles and make into strips. Join around centre section.

• Assemble quilt layers and hand or machine quilt, quilting around the outlines of the elephants and patchwork shapes.

• Bind edges of quilt with strips (straight grain) cut 12 cm [4½"] to make double binding.

Elephant

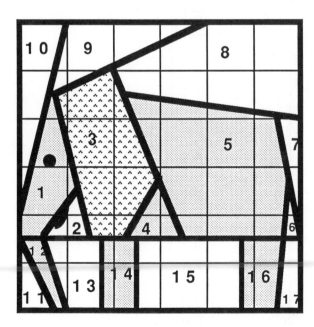

Size for quilt

24 cm [9"] square
6 × 6 squares each 4 cm [1¼"]

Colour

Gingham elephant body straight grain **1**, **4**, **5**, **12**, **14**, **16**.
Gingham elephant ear bias grain **3**.
Background **2**, **6**, **7**, **8**, **9**, **10**, **11**, **13**, **15**, **17**.

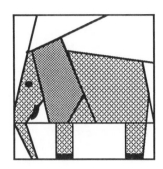

Piecing order

```
 1   1 + 2
 2   3 + 4
 3   5 + 6
 4   (5–6) + 7
 5   (5–7) + 8
 6   (1–2) + (3–4) + (5–8)
 7   (1–8) + 9
 8   (1–9) + 10
 9   11 + 12 + 13 + 14 + 15 + 16 + 17
10   (1–10) + (11–17)
```
Embroider eye, tusk, toes and tail.

> *For other projects the block may be made in a different size e.g. 30 cm [12"]. Each square, 5 cm [1¼"].*

Sheep on Clover Quilt

Some very contented sheep graze on clover.
For luck, one clover has four leaves.

Finished size

107.5 × 85 cm [43 × 34″] not including binding.

Requirements

• White for sheep 40 cm [16″].

• Light brown for heads, ears and legs 20 cm [8″].

• Background for sheep and outside border, 1 m [1¼ yd].

• Green for sashing strips, binding and applique clovers, 70 cm [¾ yd].

• Green print for ground and sashing squares, 20 cm [8″].

• Brown embroidery thread to make features on sheep and green thread for clover.

• Batting, 120 × 95 cm [48 × 38″].

• Backing fabric, 1.2 m [1¼ yd].

Cut out

• Sheep blocks 20 cm [8″] square, see page 52. Cut 11 facing left and one facing right.

• Green sashing strips. Cut 2.5 × 20 cm [1½ × 8″] wide (plus seams). Cut 31.

• Green print sashing squares. Cut 2.5 cm [1″] plus seams. Cut 20.

• Outside border strips in background colour 7.5 cm [3″] wide (plus seams).

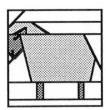

Sheep block see page 52

Construction

• Make 12 sheep blocks, (11 sheep facing left and one facing right). Embroider mouth, eyes, and a horn on one sheep.

• Cut out sashing strips and squares. Piece together into rows, and add to sheep blocks to make the centre of quilt.

• Add border.

• Trace clover pattern. Cut out clover leaves and applique in corners, making one clover with four leaves. Embroider veins and stems.

• Assemble quilt layers. Outline quilt the sheep, sashing squares and strips and clover.

• Bind quilt with strips (straight grain) cut 8 cm [3″] for double binding.

Scotty Dog Quilt

Och aye! Who could resist these
jaunty little fellows?

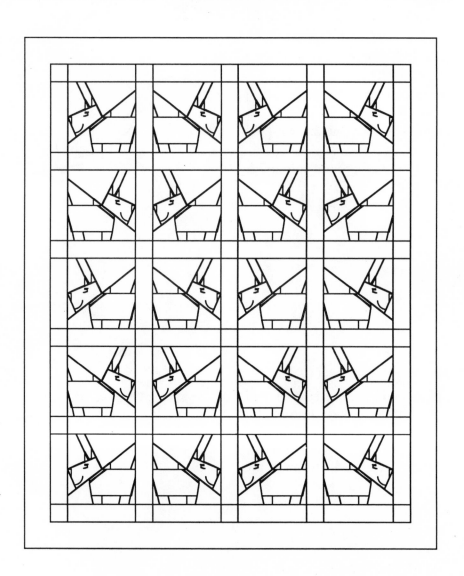

Scotty Dog quilt . Made by Kerry Gavin

Finished size

172 × 142 cm [71 × 58½″] not including binding.

Requirements

• Black for dogs, 1 m [1 yd].

• Off white for background, 1.3 m [1½ yd].

• Plaid for sashing and binding, 1.8 m [2 yd].
(note that this amount will need to be increased by
at least 1 m [40″] if sashing strips are cut on the
diagonal of the plaid)

• Red fabric for squares and outside border, 1 m
[1 yd].

• White embroidery thread for eyes.

Cut out

• 20 dog blocks, 10 facing right, 10 facing left.

• Sashing. Cut strips and squares 6 cm [2½″] wide
(plus seams).

• Border. Cut strips 8 cm [3″] wide (plus seams).

Construction

• Make 20 scotty dog blocks, *ten with templates face
down and ten with templates face up* to make the dog
face in different directions. Embroider eyes on
dogs.

• Cut squares and strips for sashing. Assemble
centre section of quilt. Add outside border (strips
will need to be joined to make length required).

• Assemble quilt layers. Outline quilt around dogs
and strips and borders.

• Bind quilt with strips of plaid (either cut straight
or bias grain to match the plaid sashing) cut 8 cm
[3″] to make a double binding.

Scotty Dog

Size for quilt

24 cm block [10″]
8 × 8 squares each 3 cm [1¼″]

Colour

Dog **2, 4, 6, 10, 12, 13, 15.**
Collar **8, 11.**
Background **1, 3, 5, 7, 9, 14, 16, 17.**

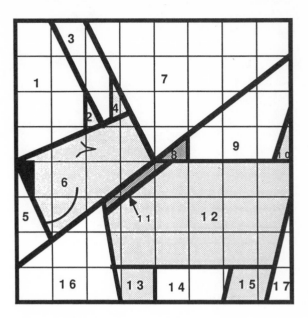

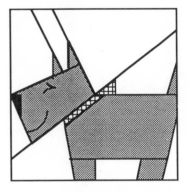

Piecing order

1   **1 + 2**
2   **3 + 4**
3   **(1−2) + (3−4)**
4   **5 + 6**
5   **(1−4) + (5−6)**
6   **(1−6) + 7**
7   **8 + 9 + 10**
8   **11 + 12**
9   **(8−10) + (11−12)**
10 **13 + 14 + 15**
11 **(8−12) + (13−15)**
12 **(8−15) + 16**
13 **(8−16) + 17**
14 **(1−7) + (8−17)**

Embroider or use button for eye. Embroider nose
and mouth, if desired.

*For other projects the block may be made in a
different size e.g. 20 cm [8″]. Each square,
2.5 cm [1″].*

Sheep on clover: a flock of sheep to count at bedtime and a four leafed clover for
good luck! (p 80). Made by Margaret Barclay

Zoo Quilt

Children love to visit the zoo and see the animals. Ours is a fragile planet, and learning about animals can teach us about the precious earth we share.

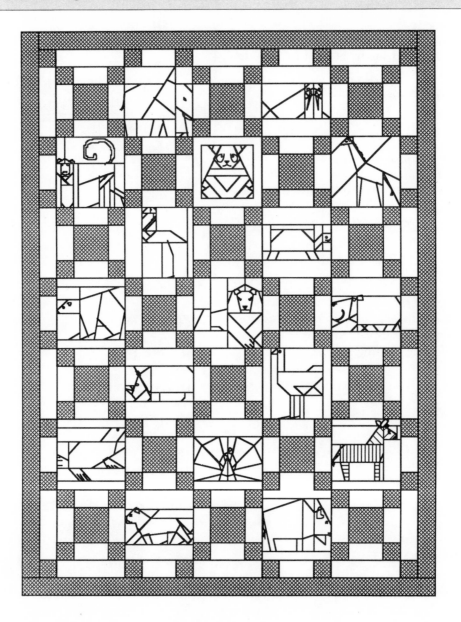

Finished size

192 × 144 cm [80 × 60″] not including binding.
7 × 5 blocks; 18 nine patch and 17 animal blocks.
Each block 24 cm [10″]

Requirements

• Blue print for nine patches, border and binding
2.3 m [2½ yd].

• Background fabric for animals and nine patches
2.3 m [2½ yd].

• Assortment of small pieces of fabric appropriate
for each animal (see instructions for each animal).

• Assortment of coloured embroidery threads as
required for details on animals.

• Batting 210 × 160 cm [90 × 70″].

• Backing 3.3 m [3¾ yd].

Template patterns for nine patch blocks and pieced border

Add seam allowances.

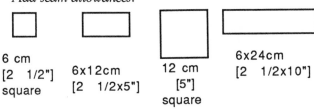

6 cm
[2 1/2"]
square

6x12cm
[2 1/2x5"]

12 cm
[5"]
square

6x24cm
[2 1/2x10"]

Construction

• Make the animal blocks in the sizes given. Add
extra strips of background fabric where necessary
to make the block up to 24 cm [10″] square.
Embroider and applique features on animals (some
features extend beyond the block and will have to
be done after the blocks are joined together).

• Make nine patch blocks.

• Join animal and nine patch blocks together as per
quilt plan. Finish embroidery.

• Piece the inside border, and add to centre section.
Add outside border.

• Mark a pattern of concentric circles into nine
patches and borders.

• Assemble quilt layers. Outline quilt around
animals and quilt marked patterns.

• Bind quilt with strips (straight grain) cut 8 cm
[3″] for double binding.

Polar Bear

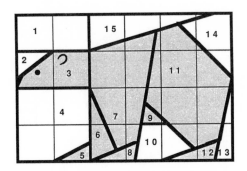

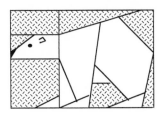

Size for quilt

16 × 24 cm [6 × 9″]
4 × 6 squares each 4 cm [1½″]

Colour

White bear **3, 5, 6, 7, 8, 9, 11, 12**.
Background **1, 2, 4, 10, 13, 14, 15**.

Piecing order

1 **2 + 3**
2 **1 + (2–3) + 4 + 5**
3 **6 + 7**
4 **(6–7) + 8**
5 **9 + 10**
6 **(9–10) + 11**
7 **(9–11) + 12**
8 **(9–12) + 13**
9 **(9–13) + 14**
10 **(6–8) + (9–14)**
11 **(6–14) + 15**
12 **(1–5) + (6–15)**

Applique ear, embroider nose and eye.

*For other projects the block may be made in a
different size e.g. 20 × 30 cm [8 × 12″]. Each
square, 5 cm [2″].*

Monkey

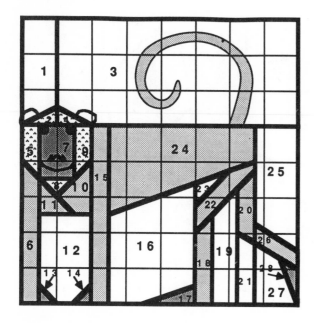

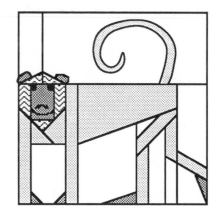

Size for quilt

24 cm [10″] square
8 × 8 squares each 3 cm [1¼″]

Colour

Dark brown monkey face, paws etc. **7, 13, 14, 17, 28**, ears.
Brown monkey ruff **2, 4, 5, 8, 9**.
Light brown monkey body **6, 10, 11, 15, 18, 20, 22, 24, 26**, tail.
Background **1, 3, 12, 16, 19, 21, 23, 25, 27**.

Piecing order

 1   **1 + 2**
 2   **3 + 4**
 3   **(1–2) + (3–4)**
Make tail from bias rouleau 1 cm [⅜″] wide and
stitch onto Piece **3**
 4   **5 + 6**
 5   **7 + 8 + 9**
 6   **(7–9) + 10**
 7   **(7–10) + 11**
 8   **12 + 13 + 14**
 9   **(7–11) + (12–14)**
10   **16 + 17**
11   **20 + 21**
12   **18 + 19 + (20–21)**
13   **(18–21) + 22 + 23**
14   **(16–17) + (18–23)**
15   **(16–23) + 24**
16   **27 + 28**
17   **25 + 26 + (27–28)**
18   **(5–6) + (7–14) + 15 + (16–24) + (25–28)**
19   **(1–4) + (5–28)**
Applique ears, embroider eyes, nostrils and mouth.

> *For other projects the block may be made in a different size e.g. 32 cm [12″] square. Each square, 4 cm [1½″].*

Elephant

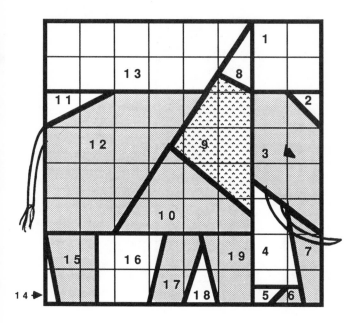

Size for quilt

24 cm square [10″]
8 × 8 squares each 3 cm [1¼″]

Colour

Grey elephant body **3, 6, 7, 10, 12, 15, 17, 19**.
Grey print ear **9**.
Background **1, 2, 4, 5, 8, 11, 13, 14, 16, 18**.

Piecing order

1   **2 + 3**
2   **5 + 6**
3   **4 + (5–6)**
4   **(4–6) + 7**
5   **1 + (2–3) + (4–7)**
6   **8 + 9 + 10**
7   **11 + 12**
8   **(11–12) + 13**
9   **(8–10) + (11–13)**
10 **14 + 15 + 16 + 17 + 18**
11 **(14–18) + 19**
12 **(8–13) + (14–19)**
13 **(1–7) + (8–19)**

Embroider tusk and eye. Make tail from rouleau with tassel end.

> For other projects the block may be made in a different size e.g. 32 cm [12″] square. Each square, 4 cm [1½″].

Flamingo

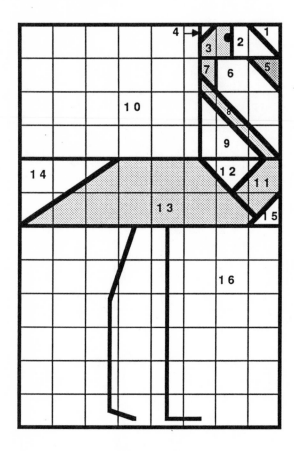

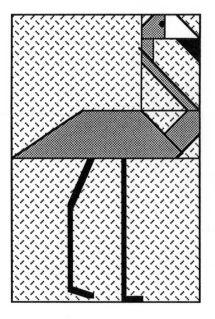

Size for quilt

24 × 16 cm [9 × 6″]
12 × 8 squares each 2 cm [¾″]

Colour

Black beak tip **5**.
White beak centre **2**.
Pink flamingo body **3**, **7**, **8**, **11**, **13**, legs.
Background **1**, **4**, **6**, **9**, **10**, **12**, **14**, **15**, **16**.

Piecing order

1   **1 + 2 + 3 + 4**
2   **5 + 6 + 7**
3   **(5–7) + 8 + 9**
4   **(1–4) + (5–9)**
5   **(1–9) + 10**
6   **11 + 12**
7   **(11–12) + 13 + 14**
8   **(11–14) + 15**

Make length of rouleau 6 mm [¼″] wide, for legs and feet. Applique onto Piece **16**.

9   **(1–10) + (11–15) + 16**

Embroider eye.

For other projects the block may be made in a different size e.g. 30 × 20 cm [12 × 9″]. Each square, 2.5 cm [1″].

Panda

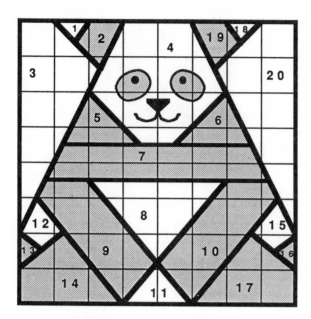

Size for quilt

20 cm [8″] square
8 × 8 squares each 2.5 cm [1″]

Colour

Black **2, 5, 6, 7, 9, 10, 13, 14, 16, 17, 19,**
eye patches.
White **4, 8, 11.**
Background **1, 3, 12, 15, 18, 20.**

Piecing order

  1 **1 + 2**
  2 **(1–2) + 3**
  3 **4 + 5 + 6**

  4 **(4–6) + 7**
  5 **8 + 9**
  6 **10 + 11**
  7 **(8–9) + (10–11)**
  8 **(4–7) + (8–11)**
  9 **12 + 13**
10 **(12–13) + 14**
11 **(4–11) + (12–14)**
12 **15 + 16**
13 **(15–16) + 17**
14 **(4–14) + (15–17)**
15 **18 + 19**
16 **(18–19) + 20**
17 **(1–3) + (4–17) + (18–20)**
Applique eye patches.
Embroider eyes, nose and mouth.

---

*For other projects the block may be made in a
different size e.g.*
24 cm [10″] square. Each square, 3 cm [1¼″].
32 cm [12″] square. Each square, 4 cm [1½″].
40 cm [16″] square. Each square, 5 cm [2″].

Rhinoceros

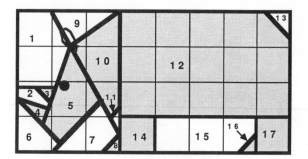

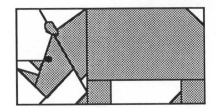

Sea Lion

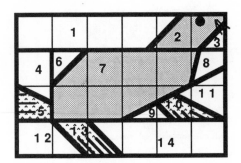

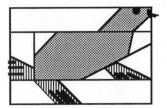

Size for quilt

12 × 24 cm [5 × 10″]
4 × 8 squares each 3 cm [1½″]

Colour

Grey rhino **3, 4, 5, 8, 10, 12, 14, 16, 17.**
Background **1, 2, 6, 7, 9, 11, 13, 15.**

Piecing order

```
 1   2 + 3
 2   1 + (2–3) + 4
 3   (1–4) + 5
 4   (1–5) + 6
 5   (1–6) + 7 + 8
 6   9 + 10 + 11
 7   (1–8) + (9–11)
 8   12 + 13
 9   14 + 15 + 16
10   (14–16) + 17
11   (12–13) + (14–17)
12   (1–11) + (12–17)
```
Embroider eye.

For other projects the block may be made in a different size e.g. 16 × 32 cm [6 × 12″]. Each square, 4 cm [1½″].

Size for quilt

16 × 24 cm [6 × 9″]
4 × 6 squares each 4 cm [1½″]

Colour

Dark brown sea lion **2, 7.**
Brown print flippers **5, 10, 13.**
Background **1, 3, 4, 6, 8, 9, 11, 12, 14.**

Piecing order

```
1   1 + 2 + 3
2   4 + 5
3   6 + 7 + 8
4   9 + 10 + 11
5   (6–8) + (9–11)
6   (4–5) + (6–11)
7   12 + 13 + 14
8   (1–3) + (4–11) + (12–13)
```
Embroider eye, lines on flippers and whiskers.

For other projects the block may be made in a different size e.g. 20 × 30 cm [8 × 12″]. Each square, 5 cm [2″].

Zoo quilt: the king of the jungle sits proudly in the middle of this magnificent quilt (p 84)

Tiger

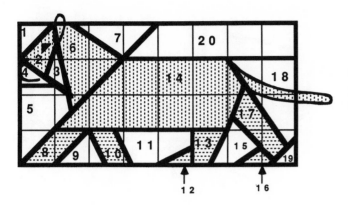

Size for quilt

12 × 24 cm [5 × 10″]
4 × 8 squares each 3 cm [1¼″]

Colour

White muzzle and ruff **3, 4**.
Orange striped tiger body; vary direction of stripes
2, 6, 8, 10, 12, 13, 14, 16, 17, tail and ear.
Background **1, 5, 7, 9, 11, 15, 18, 19, 20**.

Piecing order

1   **1 + 2 + 3**
2   **4 + 5**
3   **(1–3) + (4–5)**
4   **(1–5) + 6 + 7**
5   **8 + 9 + 10 + 11 + 12**
6   **(8–12) + 13**
7   **(8–13) + 14**
8   **15 + 16**
9   **(15–16) + 17**
10   **(8–14) + (15–17)**
Make rouleau tail and pin on Piece **18**.
11   **(8–17) + 18**
12   **(8–18) + 19**
13   **(8–19) + 20**
14   **(1–7) + (8–20)**
Applique ear, and stitch tail in place.
Embroider eye and mouth.

> *For other projects the block may be made in a different size e.g. 16 × 32 cm [6 × 12″]. Each square, 4 cm [1½″].*

With a little imagination, the designs from this book can be used to great effect on items you design yourself. Quilt created by Beth Miller; rooster, hen and chick (p 56).
Animal cushions, elephant (p 87), peacock (p 96), monkey (p 86) and cat (p 58) made by Kerry Gavin

Tortoise

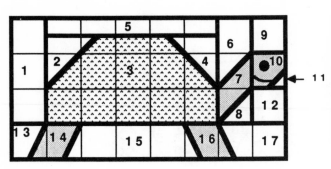

Hippo

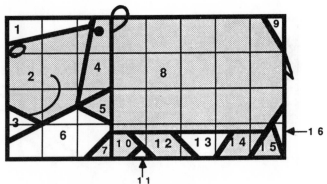

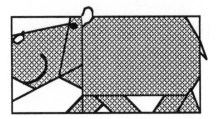

Size for quilt

12 × 24 cm [5 × 10″]
4 × 8 squares each 3 cm [1¼″]

Size for quilt

12 × 24 cm [5 × 10″]
4 × 8 squares each 3 cm [1¼″]

Colour

Brown print tortoise shell **3**.
Brown tortoise body **7, 10, 14, 16**.
Background **1, 2, 4, 5, 6, 8, 9, 11, 12, 13, 15, 17**.

Colour

Brown hippo **2, 4, 5, 7, 8, 10, 12, 14, 15**.
Background **1, 3, 6, 9, 11, 13, 16**.

Piecing order

1 **2 + 3 + 4**
2 **(2–4) + 5**
3 **6 + 7 + 8**
4 **10 + 11**
5 **9 + (10–11) + 12**
6 **1 + (2–5) + (6–8) + (9–12)**
7 **13 + 14 + 15 + 16 + 17**
8 **(1–12) + (13–17)**
Embroider eye and mouth.

Piecing order

1 **1 + 2 + 3**
2 **(1–3) + 4**
3 **5 + 6 + 7**
4 **(1–4) + (5–7)**
5 **8 + 9**
6 **10 + 11**
7 **(10–11) + 12 + 13 + 14**
8 **(8–9) + (10–14)**
9 **15 + 16**
10 **(1–7) + (8–14) + (15–16)**
Embroider nostril, mouth and eye. Applique ear and tail.

> *For other projects the block may be made in a different size e.g. 16 × 32 cm [6 × 12″]. Each square, 4 cm [1½″].*

> *For other projects the block may be made in a different size e.g. 16 × 32 cm [6 × 12″]. Each square, 4 cm [1½″].*

Lion

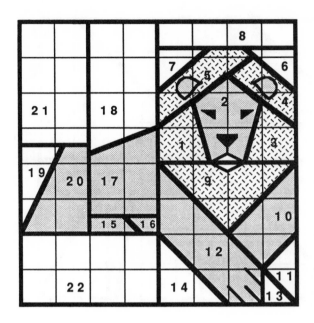

Size for quilt

24 cm [10"] square
8 × 8 squares each 3 cm [1¼"]

Colour

Yellow lion body and face **2, 10, 12, 16, 17, 20,**
and ears.
Dark yellow lion foot **15**.
Yellow print lion mane **1, 3, 4, 5, 9**.
Background **6, 7, 8, 11, 13, 14, 18, 19, 21, 22**.
Scrap of cream for muzzle.

Piecing order

1 **1 + 2 + 3**
2 **(1–3) + 4**
3 **(1–4 + 5**
4 **(1–5) + 6**
5 **(1–6) + 7**
6 **(1–7) + 8**
7 **9 + 10 + 11**
8 **12 + 13**
9 **(9–11) + (12–13) + 14**
10 **(1–8) + (9–14)**
11 **15 + 16**
12 **(15–16) + 17 + 18**
13 **19 + 20**
14 **(19–20) + 21**
15 **(15–18) + (19–21)**
16 **(15–21) + 22**
17 **(1–14) + (15–22)**
Applique ears and diamond shape for muzzle.
Embroider nose, eyes, mouth and paw.

*For other projects the block may be made in a
different size e.g. 32 cm [12"] square. Each
square, 4 cm [1½"].*

Ostrich

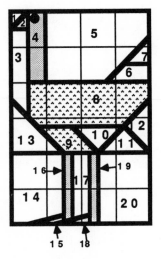 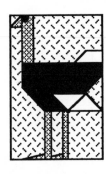

Size for quilt

24 × 16 cm [9 × 6″]
6 × 4 squares each 4 cm [1½″]

Colour

Pink head, neck and legs **2, 4, 15, 16, 18, 19.**
Black body **8, 9.**
White tail and wing **6, 10, 11.**
Background **1, 3, 5, 7, 12, 13, 14, 17, 20.**

Piecing order

    1   **1 + 2 + 3**
    2   **4 + 5**
    3   **6 + 7**
    4   **(4–5) + (6–7)**
    5   **9 + 10**
    6   **(4–7) + 8 + (9–10)**
    7   **11 + 12**
    8   **(4–10) + (11–12)**
    9   **(1–3) + (4–12)**
   10   **(1–12) + 13**
   11   **14 + 15**
   12   **(14–15) + 16 + 17**
   13   **(14–17) + 18**
   14   **(14–18) + 19 + 20**
   15   **(1–13) + (14–20)**

> *For other projects the block may be made in a
> different size e.g. 30 × 20 cm [12 × 8″]. Each
> square, 5 cm [2″].*

Giraffe

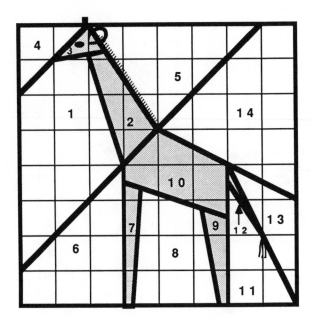

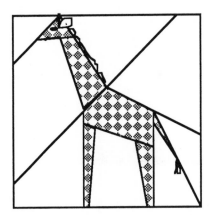

Size for quilt

24 cm square [10″]
8 × 8 squares each 3 cm [1¼″]

Colour

Yellow/brown print **2, 3, 7, 9, 10, 12.**
Background **1, 4, 5, 6, 8, 11, 13, 14.**

Piecing order

    1   **1 + 2**
    2   **(1–2) + 3**
    3   **(1–3) + 4**
    4   **(1–4) + 5**
    5   **7 + 8 + 9**

6 (7–9) + 10
7 6 + (7–10)
8 11 + 12
9 (11–12) + 13
10 (6–10) + (11–13)
11 (6–13) + 14
12 (1–5) + (6–14)

Embroider horn, eye, mane, and tassel on tail.
Applique ear from scrap of cream fabric.

*For other projects the block may be made in a
different size e.g. 32 cm [12″] square. Each
square, 4 cm [1½″].*

Zebra

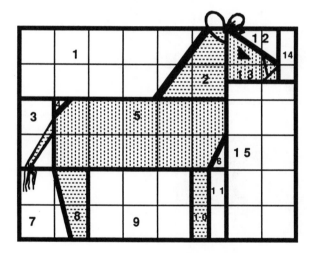

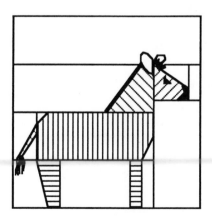

Size for quilt

18 × 24 cm [7½ × 10″]
6 × 8 squares each 3 cm [1¼″]

Colour

Striped fabric zebra body vary direction of stripes
2, 5, 8, 10, 13, tail.
Background **1, 3, 4, 6, 7, 9, 11, 12, 14, 15**.

Piecing order

1 **1 + 2**
2 **4 + 5 + 6**

Make tail out of rouleau, with stripes running
across the tail. Pin in place on piece **3**

3 **3 + (4–6)**
4 **7 + 8 + 9 + 10 + 11**
5 **(1–2) + (3–6) + (7–11)**
6 **12 + 13**
7 **(12–13) + 14**
8 **(12–14) + 15**
9 **(1–11) + (12–15)**

Applique white ears. Embroider mane (in front of
ears and line down back of neck), tail tip, nose and
eye in black.

*For other projects the block may be made in a
different size e.g. 24 × 32 cm [9 × 12″]. Each
square, 4 cm [1½″].*

Peacock

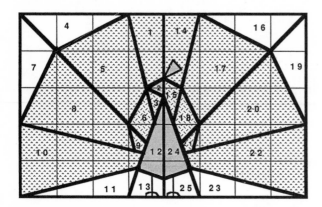

10   (14–15) + (16–18) + (19–21) + 22 + 23
11   24 + 25
12   (14–23) + (24–25)
13   (1–13) + (14–25) Press seam allowances on
this centre seam open.
Embroider crest, legs and feet.

> *For other projects the block may be made in a*
> *different size e.g. 20 × 32 cm [7½ × 12″]. Each*
> *square, 4 cm [1½″].*

Size for quilt

15 × 24 cm [6¼ × 10″]
5 × 8 squares each 3 cm [1¼″]

Colour

Turquoise print tail 1, 5, 8, 10, 14, 17, 20, 22.
Turquoise inner tail 3, 6, 9, 15, 18, 21.
Blue head and breast 2, 12, 24.
Background 4, 7, 11, 13, 16, 19, 23, 25.

Piecing order

1   1 + 2 + 3
2   4 + 5 + 6
3   7 + 8 + 9
4   (1–3) + (4–6) + (7–9) + 10 + 11
5   12 + 13
6   (1–11) + (12–13)
7   14 + 15
8   16 + 17 + 18
9   19 + 20 + 21

Bison (Buffalo)

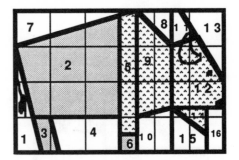

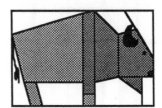

Size for quilt

16 × 24 cm [6 × 9″]
4 × 6 squares each 4 cm [1½″]

Colour

Brown Bison body 2, 3, 6.
Dark brown Bison head and shoulders 5, 9, 12,
14.
Background 1, 4, 8, 10, 11, 13, 15, 16.

Piecing order

1 3 + 4
2 2 + (3–4)
3 1 + (2–4)
4 5 + 6
5 (1–4) + (5–6)
6 (1–6) + 7
7 8 + 9 + 10
8 11 + 12
9 (11–12) + 13
10 14 + 15
11 (14–15) + 16
12 (11–13) + (14–16)
13 (1–7) + (8–10) + (11–16)
Embroider tail, eye, horn and nose.

For other projects the block may be made in a different size e.g. 20 × 30 cm [8 × 12"]. Each square, 5 cm [2"].

Colour

Brown walrus body **4, 7, 9, 10, 12, 14, 15**.
Dark brown flippers **2, 5, 17**.
Light brown muzzle **8, 13**.
Background **1, 3, 6, 11, 16**.

Piecing order

1 **1 + 2**
2 **3 + 4 + 5**
3 **(1–2) + (3–5)**
4 **6 + 7 + 8**
5 **(6–8) + 9**
Embroider tusks on pieces **10** and **15**.
6 **(6–9) + 10**
7 **11 + 12 + 13**
8 **(11–13) + 14**
9 **(11–14) + 15**
10 **(6–10) + (11–15)**
Press seam allowances on this seam open.
11 **16 + 17**
12 **(1–5) + (6–15) + (16–17)**
Embroider eyes and nostrils.

For other projects the block may be made in a different size e.g. 16 × 32 cm [6 × 12"]. Each square, 4 cm [1½"].

Walrus

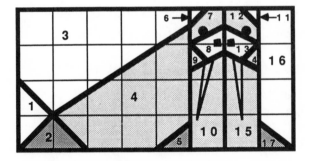

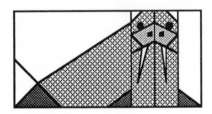

Size for quilt

12 × 24 cm [5 × 10"]
4 × 8 squares each 3 cm [1¼"]

Benjamin Bunny and Friends Quilt

Beatrix Potter's photograph of her rabbit, Benjamin, inspired this quilt.

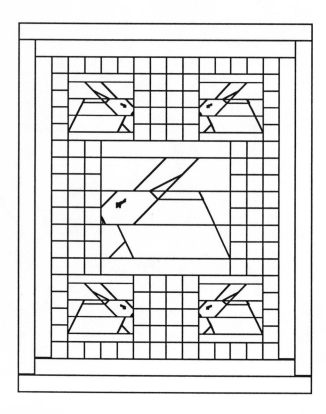

Finished size

110 × 90 cm [44 × 36″] not including binding.

Requirements

- White for rabbits and first border, 80 cm [30″].
- Bright yellow print for ground (under rabbit) and second border, 40 cm [16″].
- Blue print background for rabbits, 30 cm [12″].
- Assortment of soft yellow and blue prints to make squares, making about 90 cm [1 yd] in all.
- Extra 50 cm [20″] one blue print for binding.
- Scraps of plain blue for applique of eyes and noses.
- Blue embroidery thread for whiskers.
- Backing fabric, 120 cm [1¼ yd].
- Batting, 120 × 100 cm [48 × 40″].

Cut out

- 124 squares in print fabric each 5 cm [2″] plus seams.
- Five rabbit blocks; 1 large 40 cm [16″] square and 4 small 20 cm [8″] square.
- Inside and outside border strips 5 cm [2″] wide (plus seams).

Construction

- Make a large rabbit and 4 small rabbits. *Two of the rabbits, mark with templates face up and the the other two mark with templates face down* so that rabbits face in opposite directions.

  Applique and embroider features.

- Following the quilt plan, join the squares into

Benjamin Bunny and Friends quilt made by Ann Haddad. The bassinet quilt was made by Judy Turner (p 32)

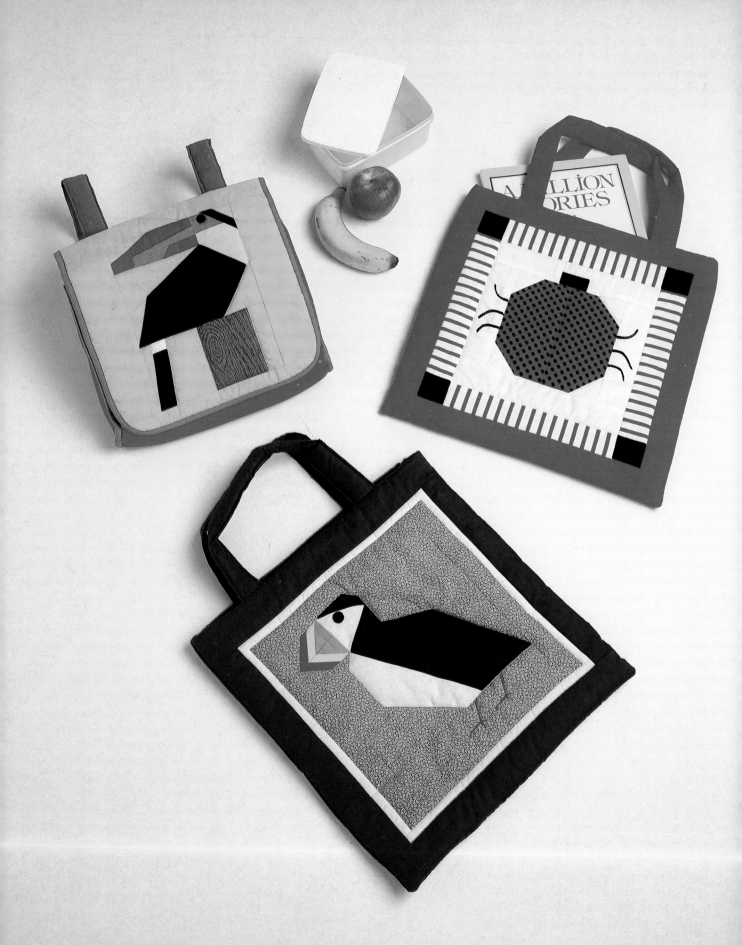

Backpack and library bags: something bright to take to school, especially for the little ones. Toucan backpack (p 112) and Puffin bag (p 109) made by Beryl Hodges. Ladybird bag (p 111) made by Kerry Gavin

Animal motifs can be used in various sizes—they make play clothes and party clothes extra special. Block designs for panda (p 89), giraffe (p 94) and ladybird (p 111). Created by Kerry Gavin

Bunnyrun quilt: ten beautiful white bunnies scamper playfully around this charming
floral quilt (p 100). Made by Beth Miller

sections, making two sections of 4 rows of 4 squares, and two sections of 8 rows of 2 squares.

Join these sections to the rabbits, then join sections to make centre of the quilt.

• Join remaining squares into strips, two strips of 16 squares for sides, and two strips of 14 squares for top and bottom. Add these around centre section.

• Add inside border, then outside border.

• Assemble quilt layers. Outline quilt rabbits and quilt a shape for back legs. Quilt a double clamshell pattern into the ground, and single clamshell pattern into background behind rabbits. Quilt squares across both diagonals, and quilt straight lines across the borders.

• Bind quilt with strips (straight grain) cut 12 cm [4½″] wide to make a double binding. When trimming the edges before binding, leave 2.5 cm [1″] of batting beyond the seam line to fill the binding.

Benjamin Bunny

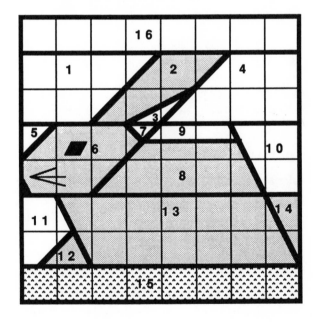

Size for quilt

Centre block 40 cm [16″] square. 8 × 8 squares. each 5 cm [2″].
Corner blocks 20 cm [8″] square. 8 × 8 squares. each 2.5 cm [1″].

Colour

White bunny **2, 6, 8, 12, 13, 14.**
Ground **11, 15.**
Background **1, 3, 4, 5, 7, 9, 10.**

Piecing order

1 **1 + 2 + 3**
2 **(1–3) + 4**
3 **5 + 6 + 7**
4 **8 + 9**
5 **(5–7) + (8–9) + 10**
6 **11 + 12**
7 **(11–12) + 13 + 14**
8 **(1–4) + (5–10) + (11–14)**
9 **(1–14) + 15 + 16**
Applique nose and eye. Embroider whiskers.

Bunnyrun Quilt

Ten white bunny rabbits scamper around a centre of simple squares.

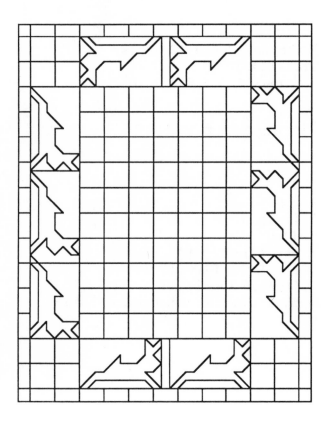

Finished size
112.5 × 90 cm [45 × 36"].

Requirements
- White fabric for bunnies, 40 cm [½ yd].
- Background behind bunnies, 50 cm [20"].
- Assortment of prints for squares, totalling 1.3 m [1½ yd].
- Pink embroidery thread for features on bunnies.
- Batting, 125 × 100 cm [50 × 40"].
- Backing fabric, 1.3 m [1½ yd].

Cut out
- Ten bunny blocks.
- 140 squares each 7.5 cm [3"] plus seams.

Construction
- Make ten bunny blocks. Embroider features.
- Sew bunnies into four strips: 2 strips of 3 bunnies; and 2 strips of 2 bunnies with a rectangle of 15 × 2.5 cm [6 × 1"] in centre.
- Cut squares. Join squares into centre section of quilt; (10 rows of 7 squares each).
- Make four corners each 2 rows of 2 squares.
- Assemble strips of bunnies to sections of squares. Join all sections.
- Add border created from rows of squares (strips of 14 squares for sides and 13 for top and bottom).
- Assemble quilt layers. Outline quilt squares and bunnies (but do not quilt outside squares).
- Trim batting and backing. Press under seam allowance on outside border of squares. Turn to back and hand stitch in place.

Bunnyrun

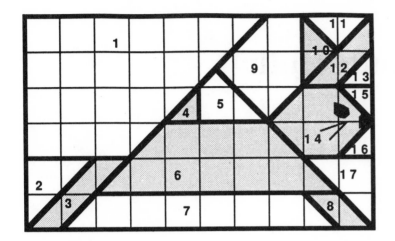
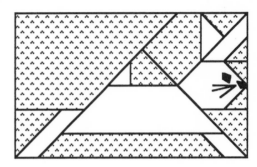

Size for quilt

15 × 25 cm [6 × 10″]
6 × 10 squares each 2.5 cm [1″]

Colour

White bunny **3, 4, 6, 8, 10, 12, 14**.
Background **1, 2, 5, 7, 9, 11, 13, 15, 16, 17**.

Piecing order

 1   **2 + 3**

 2   **1 + (2–3)**
 3   **4 + 5**
 4   **7 + 8**
 5   **(4–5) + 6 + (7–8)**
 6   **9 + 10 + 11**
 7   **12 + 13**
 8   **14 + 15 + 16**
 9   **(12–13) + (14–16) + 17**
10   **(9–11) + (12–17)**
11   **(4–8) + (9–17)**
12   **(1–3) + (4–17)**
Embroider nose, eye and whiskers.

Panda Quilt

The gentle bamboo eating panda is everyone's favourite.

Finished size

95 × 85 cm [38 × 34"] not including binding.

Requirements

- Black fabric for panda, 20 cm [8"].
- White fabric for panda, 20 cm [8"].
- Scrap of green for applique leaves.
- Green print for triangles and binding 70 cm [¾yd].
- Background fabric 1.4 m [1¾ yd].
- Light brown for bamboo border 20 cm [8"].
- Deep red for squares 8 cm [3"].
- Black embroidery thread.
- 2 small black buttons.
- Batting, 105 × 95 cm [42 × 38"].
- Backing fabric, 1.1 m [1¼ yd].

Template shapes

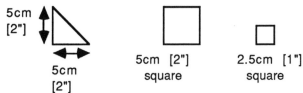

5cm [2"]

5cm [2"]

5cm [2"] square

2.5cm [1"] square

Cut out

- Panda block 40 cm [16"] square (page 89).
- Green print 96 triangles.
- Background fabric border strips and squares

5 cm [2″] wide (plus seams) and border strips 2.5 cm [1″] wide (plus seams) 96 triangles.

• Light brown print. Straight grain strips 2.5 cm [1″] wide (plus seams).

• Deep red squares cut 8 each 5 cm [2″] square and 4 each 2.5 cm [1″] square plus seams.

Panda block see page 89

Construction

• Make panda block; see page 89. Applique and embroider features and bamboo in paws and mouth. Use buttons for eyes, adding a white highlight by taking strands of white thread from buttonhole over outside of button.

• Cut out triangles from green print and background fabric. Piece together into squares.

• Using the quilt plan as a guide, calculate patterns and lengths of borders required

Working outwards from panda block, add the borders which have been pieced together from triangles and squares as indicated on the plan.

• Assemble quilt layers. Outline quilt panda, triangles and bamboo border. Quilt double lines across bamboo border at intervals, to represent the pattern of bamboo.

• Bind quilt with green print strips cut 8 cm [3″] wide to make doubled binding.

Penguin Parade Quilt

Penguins waddle up the beach to their burrows.

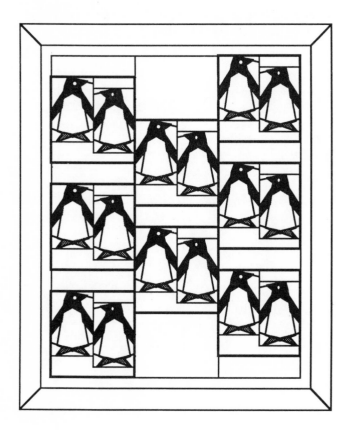

Finished size

144 × 120 cm [54 × 45"].

Requirements

• Navy blue ticking for background and outside border, 2.5 m [3 yd] (note that extra fabric is allowed for matching stripes).

• Black fabric for heads and flippers, 40 cm [½ yd].
• White fabric for bodies, 50 cm [20"].
• Red fabric for feet, and first border, 50 cm [20"].
• Batting, 160 × 130 cm [60 × 50"].
• Backing fabric, 2.6 m [3 yd].

Cut out

• Penguin blocks 24 × 16 cm [9 × 6"]. Cut 16, 8 with templates face down and 8 with templates face up to make penguins face in opposite directions. Make stripes match as much as possible.

• Rectangles of background fabric. Cut 7 each 8 × 32 cm [3 × 12"] and 2 each 24 × 32 cm [9 × 12"] plus seams.

• Red strips for inside border. Cut 4 cm [1½"] wide plus seams. Strips will need to be joined to make required lengths.

• Outside border strips 10 cm [4"] wide plus seams. Have strips horizontal for sides and vertical for top and bottom.

Construction

• Make 16 penguins, 8 facing left and 8 facing right.

• Add necessary pieces to make 8 blocks (32 cm [12"] square) with two penguins in each (see diagram). Applique eyes.

• Join the rectangles of background fabric to the penguin blocks to make three vertical sections as shown (joining 3 rectangles 8 × 32 cm [3 × 12"] to each of the first and third sections and then both 24 × 32 cm [9 × 12"] rectangles and the remaining rectangle 8 × 32 cm [3 × 12"] to centre section).

104

Join the three sections together.

• Add first border from pieced red fabric.

• Add second border, with stripes going horizontal at sides and vertical at top and bottom. Mitre corners (see page 28).

• Assemble quilt layers. Outline quilt penguins and first border. Free quilt wavy lines in centre section of quilt.

• Trim batting and backing. Press a narrow seam allowance around outside border, turn to the back of the quilt and hand stitch down.

Penguin

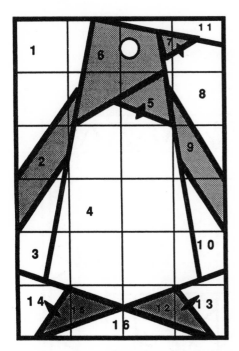

Note notches to assist in correctly orienting triangles.

Size for quilt

24 × 16 cm [9 × 6″]
6 × 4 squares each 4 cm [1½″]

Colour

Black head and flippers **2, 5, 6, 7, 9**.
White body **4**.
Red feet **12, 15**.
Background **1, 3, 8, 10, 11, 13, 14, 16**.

Piecing order

1   **1 + 2 + 3**
2   **4 + 5**
3   **(4–5) + 6**
4   **7 + 8 + 9 + 10**
5   **(1–3) + (4–6) + (7–10)**
6   **(1–10) + 11**
7   **12 + 13**
8   **(1–11) + (12–13)**
9   **14 + 15 + 16**
10   **(1–13) + (14–16)**

Applique or embroider eye.

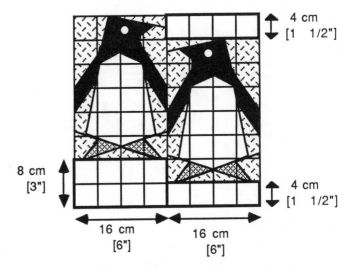

Two penguins assembled in 32 cm [12″] block.

Polar Bear Wall Hanging

Mother bear looks after her twin babies under the coloured streamers of the aurora.

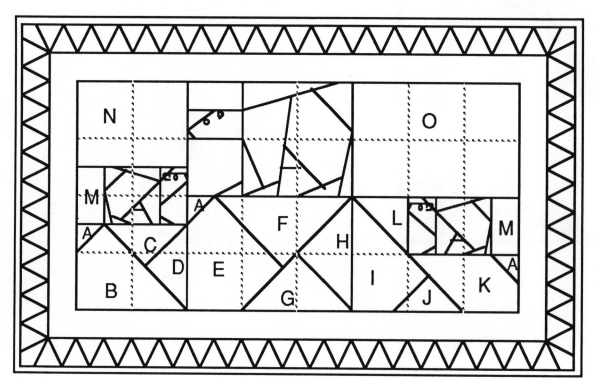

Scale: 1 square = 10 cm [4″]

Pretty polar bears play in the snow and ice, but baby will be snug under this cot quilt of simple squares (p 33) made by Judy Tuner.

Finished size

60 × 100 cm [24 × 40″] not including binding.

Template shapes for border

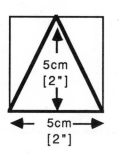
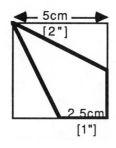

Template shapes for snow and small background areas

Snow areas: one square 10 cm [4″]. Shaded areas indicate sky colours.

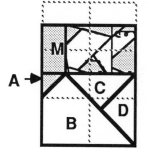
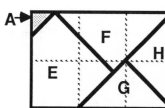

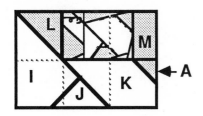

Requirements

• Blue fabric for sky, triangles in border and binding 40 cm [½ yd].
• Aqua, pale blue and lavender fabric for sky and triangles in border 20 cm [8″] each colour.
• White fabric for polar bears and borders 50 cm [20″].
• Scraps of white textured fabrics for snow areas.
• Black embroidery thread for features.
• Batting, 70 × 110 cm [28 × 44″].
• Backing fabric, 70 cm [¾ yd].

Cut out

• Cut two strips (selvedge to selvedge) from each of the blue, aqua and lavender fabrics. Cut the strips in random sizes, from 2.5 cm [1″] to 6 cm [2½″] wide. Join strips to make one piece of fabric, and press. Use this fabric to make sky background, including background behind bears, piece N, 15 × 20 cm [6 × 8″] plus seams, piece O, 20 × 30 cm [8 × 12″].
• Polar bear blocks. (See page 85). Mother 20 × 30 cm [8 × 12″]. Baby 10 × 15 cm [4 × 6″], cut 2, one facing each way.
• Snow areas from the illustrated templates.
• White border strips 5 cm [2″] wide plus seams.
• Border triangles. Cut 56 coloured triangles. Cut 60 white triangles and 4 corner shapes.
• Blue binding strips (straight grain) 7 cm [2¾″] wide.

Construction

• Piece mother polar bear and baby polar bear blocks making sure the baby bears face opposite directions. Applique and embroider features.
• Piece snow areas, making three sections.

Bedtime a circus? Gorgeous gingham elephants for a cot quilt and bumper (p 78)

- Complete the three sections of the quilt by adding the mother bear to the centre section and sky areas to both side sections. Do not try to match the strips; deliberately mistmatch them.

- Add first border of white fabric.

- Piece coloured and white triangles into strips for the second border, making four strips. Add the corner shapes to the top and bottom strips. Stitch strips to the white border, treating the corners in a similar way to a mitre, (i.e. do not sew across seam allowances at the corners (see page 29).

- Assemble quilt layers, and hand or machine quilt. Free quilt a pattern into the sky areas, and outline quilt bears, snow areas, and borders.

- Bind edges of quilt with strips to make doubled binding.

Mother polar bear (see p. 85)

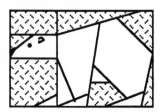

Polar Bear Baby

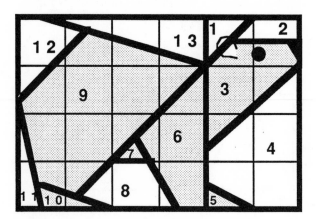

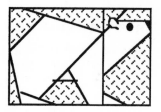

Size for quilt

10 × 15 cm [4 × 6″]
4 × 6 squares each 2.5 cm [1″]

Colour

White **3, 5, 6, 7, 9, 10**
Background **1, 2, 4, 8, 11, 12, 13.**

Piecing order

  1 2 + 3
  2 1 + (2−3) + 4 + 5
  3 7 + 8
  4 6 + (7−8)
  5 (6−8) + 9
  6 (6−9) + 10
  7 (6−10) + 11
  8 (6−10) + 12
  9 (6−12) + 13
10 (1−5) + (6−13)
Embroider eye, nose and ear.

Puffin Bag

Library bags are always in demand. A puffin is a most appropriate motif, but any of the block designs could be used instead.

Finished size

40 cm [16"] square.

Requirements

• Small pieces of red, yellow, pale blue and black fabric to make the puffin.

• White for puffin and middle border, 12 cm [5"].
• Blue print for background of puffin and inside border, 20 cm [¼ yd].
• Plain blue fabric for outside border, back, lining and handles, 80 cm [1 yd].
• Batting, 50 cm [20"].
• Backing fabric for quilting, 50 cm [20"].

Construction

• Make puffin block. Add borders:
a. Cut inside border strips 3 cm [1"] wide plus seams from background fabric.
b. Cut middle border strips 1 cm [½"] wide plus seams from white fabric.
c. Cut outside border strips 4 cm [1½"] wide from blue fabric.

• Cut backing fabric and batting into squares 2.5 cm [1"] larger than finished block. Assemble layers, and machine quilt around puffin and borders. Straight stitch close to edges and trim.

• Cut bag back from blue fabric 40 cm [16"] square (plus seams). Cut batting slightly larger. Pin together.

• Pin patchwork front and back of bag together, right sides inside. Machine stitch around three sides. Trim and turn right side out.

• Cut out handles 8 × 46 cm [3 × 18"] (plus seams). Press under seam allowances, then press in half lengthwise. Cut batting strips 4 × 46 cm [1½ × 18"] and slip into fold. Machine stitch down both edges of handles. Pin and stitch handles onto bag.

• Cut lining pieces 40 cm [16″] square (plus seams). Pin together and stitch down both sides and part way across the bottom, leaving 16 cm [6″] open for turning. Do not turn right side out.

• Slip lining over bag (right sides will be together), pin and stitch together. Turn bag through opening, and slip stitch opening closed.

• Push lining into bag, then sew a line of stitching a little distance down from the top of the bag to hold lining in place.

Puffin

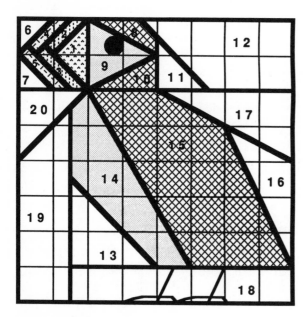

Size for bag

24 cm [10″]
8 × 8 squares each 3 cm [1¼″]

Colour

Blue **1**.
Yellow **2, 3**.
Red **4, 5**, legs.
Black **8, 10, 15**.
White **9, 14**.
Background **6, 7, 11, 12, 13, 16, 17, 18, 19, 20**.

Piecing order

1   **1 + 2**
2   **(1−2) + 3**
3   **(1−3) + 4**
4   **(1−4) + 5**
5   **(1−5) + 6 + 7**
6   **8 + 9 + 10**
7   **(8−10) + 11**
8   **(8−11) + 12**
9   **(1−7) + (8−12)**
10   **13 + 14 + 15 + 16**
11   **(13−16) + 17**
12   **(13−17) + 18**
13   **(13−18) + 19**
14   **(13−19) + 20**
15   **(1−12) + (13−20)**
Embroider eye and red legs.

Bag: (Note: no seams allowed)

Front   Back   Handles

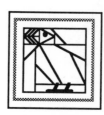

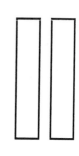

40 cm [16″]
square

40 cm [16″]
square

8 x 46 cm
[3 x 18″]

Ladybird

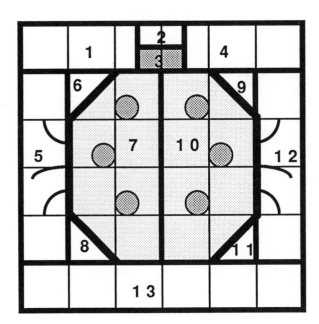

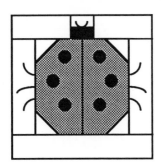

Size for bag

24 cm [9″] square
6 × 6 squares each 4 cm [1½″]

Colour

Black **3**.
Red with black spots **7, 10**.
Background **1, 2, 4, 5, 6, 8, 9, 11, 12, 13**.

Ladybird Bag

Finished size

40 cm [15″] square

Requirements

• Red and black spotted fabric for ladybird, 10 cm [4″].
• White fabric for background of block, 10 cm [4″].
• Scraps of black fabric for ladybird's head and corner squares of border.
• Red and white striped fabric for border 8 cm [3″].
• Red fabric for outside border, back, lining and handles 80 cm [1 yd].
• Batting, 50 cm [20″].
• Backing fabric for quilting 50 cm [20″].

Bag: *No seams allowed*

Front	Back	Handles

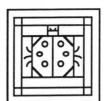 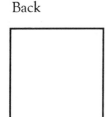 

40 cm [15"] square	40 cm [15"] square.	
24 cm [9"] block		8 x 46cm
with two 4 cm		[3 x 18"].
[1 1/2"] borders.		

Piecing order

1 **2 + 3**
2 **1 + (2−3) + 4**
3 **6 + 7 + 8**
4 **9 + 10 + 11**
5 **5 + (6−8) + (9−11) + 12**
6 **(1−4) + (5−12) + 13**
Embroider legs and feelers.

Construction

Construct as for Puffin bag varying borders as illustrated in diagram.

> *For other projects the block may be made in a different size e.g. 15 cm [6″]. Each square, 2.5 cm [1″].*

Toucan Backpack

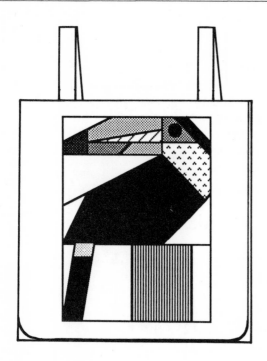

A bright and useful bag for a young child on the move.

Finished size

30 cm [12″] square.

Requirements

• Yellow for back flap, background of block and lining, 70 cm [¾ yd].

• Red for body of bag and gussets, 40 cm [½ yd].

• Blue for binding, 30 cm [12″].

• Green for straps, 20 cm [¼ yd].

• Small pieces of black, white, paler yellow, orange and brown for toucan (also use scraps of pieces from main part of the bag).

• Thin firm batting, 50 × 80 cm [20 × 32″].

• 2 Buckles or 4 D-rings.

Construction

• Make toucan block with background of bright yellow.

• Add borders to make block 30 cm [12″] square (plus 1 cm [⅜″] seam.

• Cut red fabric into gussets and main part of bag, as shown in diagram, allowing 1 cm [⅜″] for seams all around. Join red section of bag to toucan block (bag flap).

• Cut lining for gussets and bag from yellow fabric, allowing generous 2 cm [¾″] seam allowances.

  Cut batting for interlining the same size.

• Pin rectangle of bag body to corresponding batting and lining pieces.

• Machine quilt around toucan.

  Straight stitch close to all edges. Trim away excess batting and backing.

• Cut straps from green fabric, adding narrow seam allowances.

  Press under seam allowances on edges, then press straps in half lengthwise.

  Cut batting 4 cm [1½″] wide and the length of straps. Slip batting into fold, and machine stitch around edges to hold batting in place.

  Fold one end of each strap back 3 cm [1¼″] to

make loops for buckles, insert buckle (or 2 D-rings) and stitch loop closed.

Pin mark 25 cm [10"] from bottom of each loop. Pin straps onto body of bag, 5 cm [2"] from sides and placing marker pins 1 cm [⅜"] down from the top of bag (where the yellow flap meets the red body of the bag). Stitch straps to bag, stitching down to the buckle loops.

• Pin batting and lining to gusset pieces. Straight stitch around the edges, and trim.

• Cut blue fabric into bias strips 6 cm [2½"] wide. Join strips together to make 2.7 m [3 yd] bias. Press in half lengthwise to make double binding.

• Bind top of gusset edges and inside edge of bag.

• Pin gussets to main body of bag, right sides outside. Stitch gussets to bag, stitching from the gusset side, and rounding corners slightly. Trim.

• Bind remaining edges of bag, rounding the corners of the flap.

If binding is to be machine finished, stitch it to the lining side of the bag, fold over, and machine stitch on the outside.

For hand finishing, machine stitch bias to the right side, fold over and hand stitch in place.

Colour

Red **5**.
Green **1, 4**.
Blue **3, 12**.
Orange **2**.
Yellow **13**.
White **17**.
Black **8, 11, 14, 18**.
Perch **20**.
Background **6, 7, 9, 10, 15, 16, 19, 21**.

Piecing order

1 **1 + 2**
2 **3 + 4**
3 **(1−2) + (3−4)**
4 **(1−4) + 5**
5 **(1−5) + 6**
6 **7 + 8**
7 **(7−8) + 9**
8 **(1−6) + (7−9)**
9 **12 + 13**
10 **10 + 11 + (12−13) + 14**
11 **(10−14) + 15**
12 **(1−9) + (10−15)**
13 **17 + 18**
14 **16 + (17−18) + 19 + 20 + 21**
15 **(1−15) + (16−21)**
Applique circle for eye.

Toucan

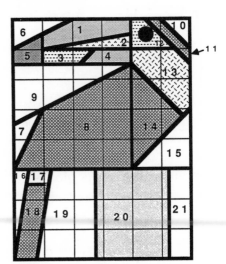

Size for backpack

24 × 18 cm [10 × 7½"] block
8 × 6 squares each 3 cm [1¼"]

Backpack: (Note: no seams allowed)

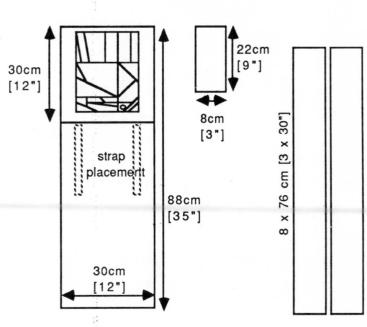

Bag   Gusset   Handles

30cm [12"]

strap placement

88cm [35"]

30cm [12"]

22cm [9"]

8cm [3"]

8 × 76 cm [3 × 30"]

Ele's Embroidered Quilt

Charming and feminine, this quilt effectively combines simple patchwork with simple embroidery. Designed and created by Wendy Saclier and Vivienne Mildren.

Finished size

183 × 136 cm [74½ × 55½"]
7 × 5 blocks each 20 cm [8"].

Requirements

• Pink fabric for sashing and binding, 2 m [2¼ yd].
• Cream fabric for background of embroidered blocks, patchwork blocks and second border 2 m [2¼ yd].
• Cream and pink print for patchwork blocks and first border 1.5 m [1¾ yd].
• Assortment of stranded embroidery threads in pinks, apricot, lavender, soft green, aqua, fawn and yellows (or colours to tone in with chosen pink print fabric).
• Batting, 146 × 194 cm [60 × 80"].
• Backing fabric, 3 m [3½ yd].

Ele's embroidered quilt. This could become a lovely heirloom for the girls in the family. Created by Vivienne Mildren and Wendy Saclier

Here are eight just perfect pairs of penguins marching on parade (p 104). Made by Beth Miller

Advent Calendar: a splendid way to count the days until Christmas. Each little red door hides a cross-stitched surprise (p 132). Designed by Linda McGuire

Hang this quilt on the wall and join in the fun of a day with busy Miss Mouse (p 118). Designed by Beverley Sach. Made by Pam Taylor

Template shapes (add seam allowances)

Block size – 20 cm [8″]

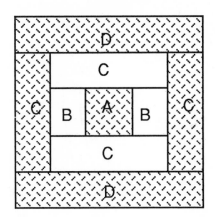

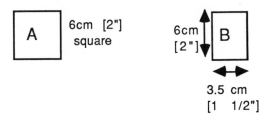

A 6cm [2″] square

6cm [2″] B

3.5 cm [1 1/2″]

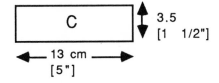

C

3.5 [1 1/2″]

13 cm [5″]

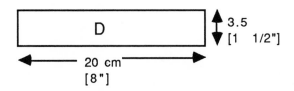

D

3.5 [1 1/2″]

20 cm [8″]

Centre square – 6 cm [2″]
Strips – 3.5 cm [1½″]

Cut out

• 18 patchwork blocks:
Pink print from template A, 18
Cream from template B, 36
Cream from template C, 36
Print from template C, 36
Print from template D, 36

• Cut 17 squares of cream fabric, each 20 cm [8″] square plus seam allowances.

• Sashing in pink fabric, 3.5 cm [1½″] wide plus seams.

• Inside border in print fabric, 3.5 cm [1½″] wide plus seams.

• Outside border in cream fabric, 4 cm [1¾″].

Construction

• Trace flower designs onto cream squares, using the designs given. Embroider the designs, changing the colours and adapting the designs freely so that each block is slightly different. You may like to embroider the girl's name in the centre block, as in the original.

• Make 18 patchwork blocks, constructing each block in log cabin fashion (courthouse steps variation).

• Join blocks to pink sashing strips to make quilt centre.

• Add inside border of pink print fabric (joins will be necessary to make length required). Add outside border of cream fabric.

• Mark a heart quilting design around embroidered motifs.

• Assemble quilt layers and hand quilt. Outline quilt patchwork shapes and borders. Quilt hearts.

• Bind edges with strips (straight grain), cut 8 cm [3″] wide to make double binding.

Miss Mouse Quilt

Miss Mouse is a busy creature as she helps with the shopping and looks after her numerous nieces and nephews. A truly delightful wall hanging in machine applique. Designed by Beverley Sach.

Finished size

119 × 88 cm [48 × 35½"].

Requirements

• White spotted fabric for background of blocks, 60 cm [¾ yd].

• Pink print for sashing, 60 cm [¾ yd] (this quantity allows for vertical stripes).

• Deep pink print for border and binding, 1.3 m [1½ yd].

• Assortment of small pieces of print and plain fabrics for applique, including grey for mouse, white, pink and blue prints for dresses, etc.

• Pink satin ribbon 1 cm [⅜"] wide for bows, 1.5 m [1¾ yd].

• Blue satin ribbon 1 cm [⅜"] wide for bows, 80 cm [1 yd].

• Assortment of embroidery threads in blues, pinks, grey and soft green for embroidering details, flowers, etc.

• Machine embroidery thread in colours to match fabrics.

• Lace for outside border, 4.5 m [5 yd].

• Assortment of small scraps of lace for applique.

• Batting, 1.3 m × 1 m [52 × 40"].

• Backing fabric, 1.3 m [1½ yd].

Cut out

• Background blocks 25 cm [10"] square.

• Sashing strips. Cut 6 cm [2½"] wide.

• Outside border. Cut strips 10 cm [4"] wide plus seams.

• Strips 8 cm [3"] wide (straight grain) for binding.

Construction

• Trace applique designs. The designs were too large to fit on one page, and are spread over two pages.

• Using the traced designs as your patterns, machine applique the designs, following the general instructions for machine applique (see page 20).

Special effects

Bicycle wheels and rocking chairs. Make fine rouleau, (see page 21), press flat, then curve into shape and tack (baste) in place. Machine stitch with small straight stitches.

Kite. Leave kite until sashing is joined to blocks, then applique and embroider it on.

Bows. Make bows from satin ribbon, and stitch onto quilt.

• Embroider details, flowers, wool, etc., using simple embroidery (see page 22).

• Cut sashing strips and join blocks and sashing together. Complete kite.

• Add outside border.

• Assemble quilt layers and outline quilt around blocks and borders. Leave applique unquilted.

• Pin lace around outside edge of border.

• Bind edges with strips (straight grain) to make double binding.

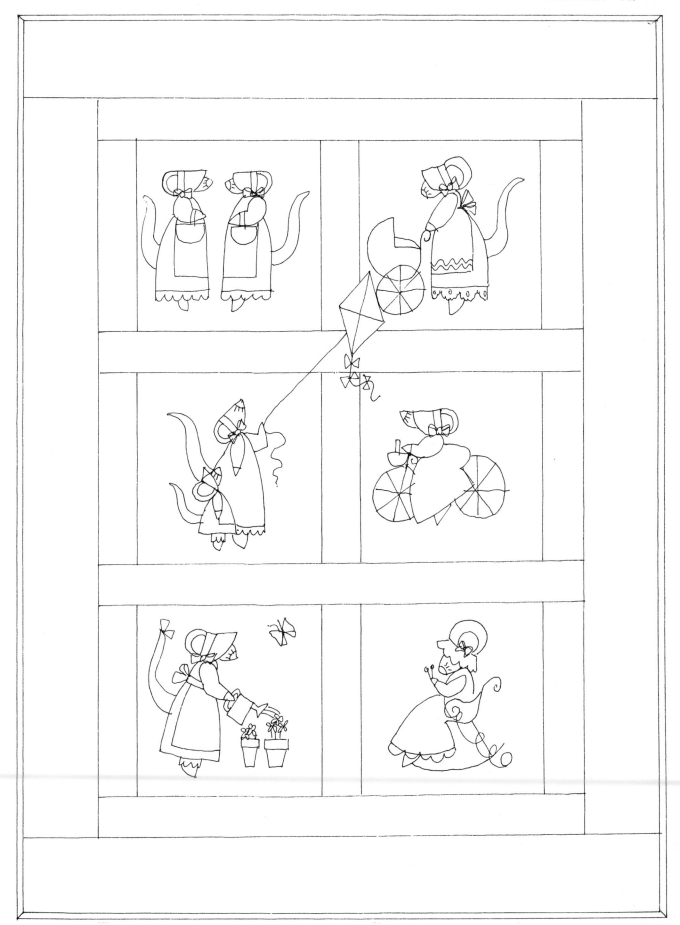

• Gather lace for cap frill and skirt frill before attaching them.

• The cap bow is attached separately.

• The rocking chair is made from a rouleau.

• The wool is embroidered in either chain or stem stitch.

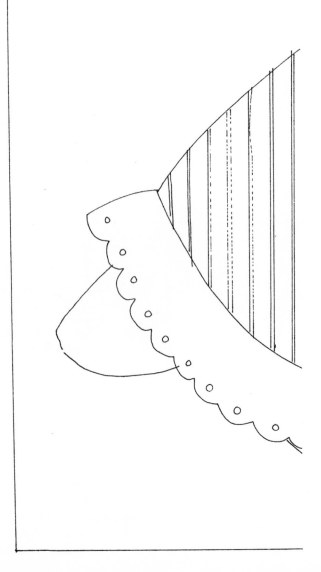

• Sew the kite on when blocks are joined together (see drawing of completed quilt for placement).

• The bows on the kite and mouse are attached separately.

• The little hand embroidered flowers are optional.

• The kite string is embroidered in either chain or stem stitch.

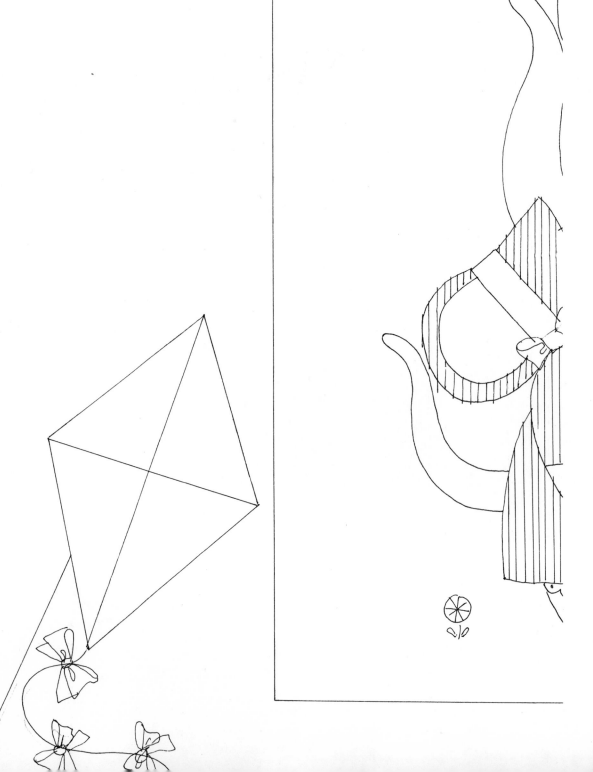

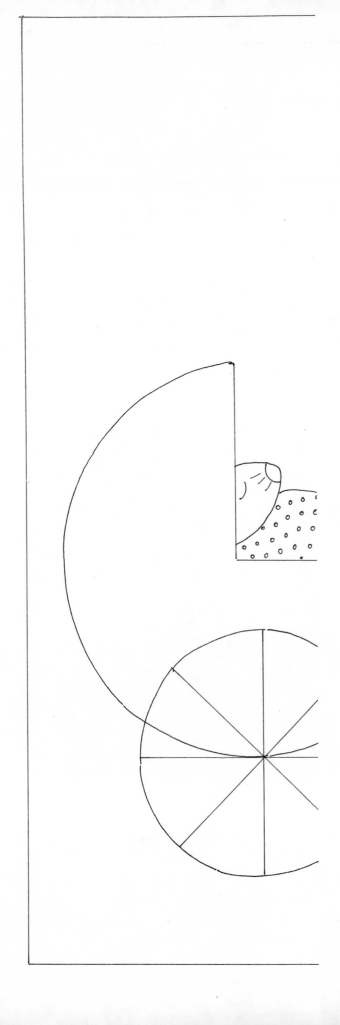

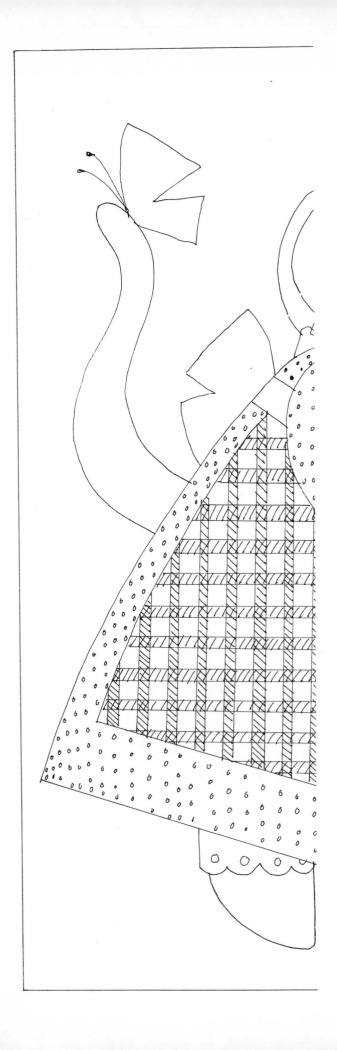

• The bicycle frame and wheels are made in rouleau.

• The bow on the bonnet is attached separately.

• Chain stitch leaves on fruit.

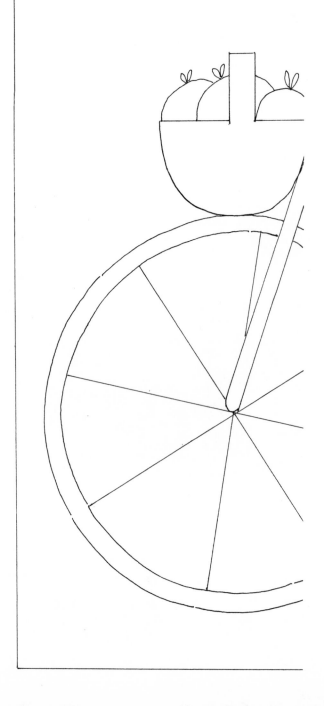

• The bonnet bows are attached separately.

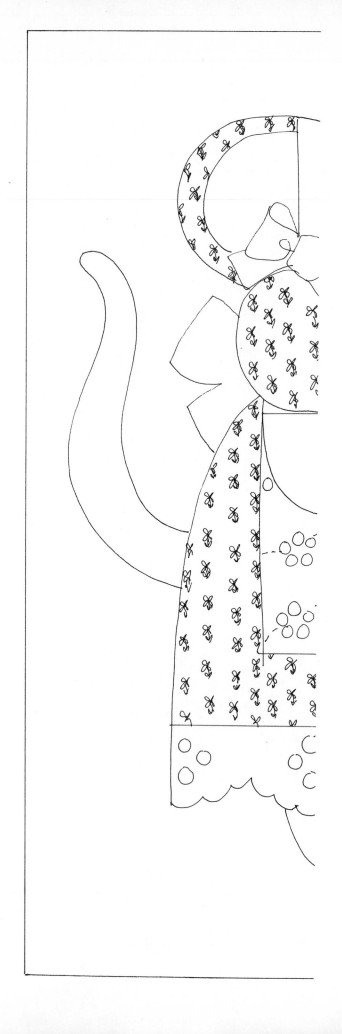

Advent Calendar Quilt

This calendar could become a treasured part of a family Christmas tradition. It is made in the log cabin design with a special surprise; the centre squares are little doors that open onto cross stitch motifs. Designed and created by Linda McGuire.

Finished size

120 × 80 cm [48 × 32″] not including binding.

Requirements

• 45 × 30 cm [12 × 18″] linen, 28 threads per 2.5 cm [1″].

• Stranded embroidery threads in red, green, black, yellow, blue, pink, brown, light brown, orange, purple, beige, and gold.

• Fabrics for strips – 3 dark toned red and green prints and 3 light toned red and green prints.
First dark print fabric, 20 cm [8″].
First light print fabric, 25 cm [10″]
Second dark print fabric, 30 cm [12″]
Second light print fabric, 35 cm [14″]
Third dark print fabric, 40 cm [16″]
Third light print fabric, 45 cm [18″]

• Fabric for binding, 40 cm [½ yd] dark toned print.

• Fabric for doors and binding 1.2 m [1½ yd] plain red fabric.

• Batting, 90 × 130 cm [36 × 52″].

• Backing fabric, 1.3 m [1½ yd].

• 24 buttons or little bells.

Construction

• Embroider the cross stitch centre squares. Firstly stop the outside edges of the piece of linen fraying by machining a row of zigzag stitching around the edges.
Mark the linen into 24 squares by placing lines of tacking (basting) at 7 cm [2¾″] intervals. Embroider the cross stitch motifs, following charts and using two strands of embroidery thread.
Cut the linen into 6.2 cm [2½″] squares (includes seam allowances around 5 cm [2″] squares).

• Make the doors. Cut 48 squares of red fabric each 5 cm [2″] plus seams. Stitch pairs of squares together, stitching around only three sides. Trim corners and turn right side out. Press.

• Cut light and dark prints into strips 2.5 cm [1″] wide plus seams.

• Sew strips to centre squares to make log cabin blocks, placing the doors correctly for each block as indicated in diagram. Note that the doors do not go in the same place in each block; the door must go below the centre square.
Begin each block with the first dark strip. Once the door is sewn in, be careful not to catch it when you are sewing the other strips.

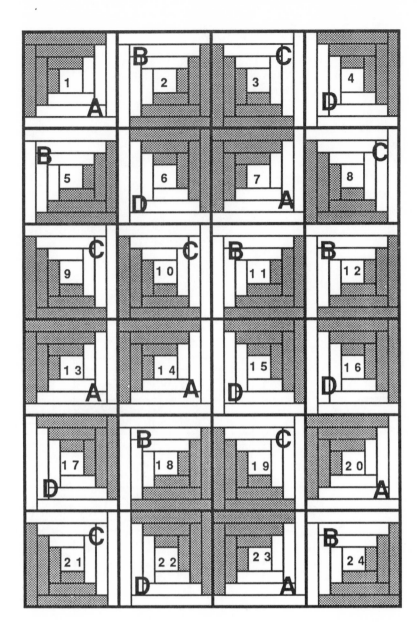

Blocks
1   Wreath
2   Christmas tree
3   Decorations
4   Bell
5   Drummer
6   Snowman
7   Poinsettia
8   Partridge in a
    pear tree
9   Holly
10 Candy Cane
11 Plum pudding
12 Stocking
13 Presents
14 Santa
15 Reindeer
16 Sleigh
17 Candles
18 Church
19 Carols
20 Star
21 Wise men
22 Angel
23 Shepherd
24 Navtivity

• Stitch blocks together, 6 rows of 4 blocks, following the layout given the diagram of of the quilt design.

• Assemble quilt layers and outline quilt strips and centre squares.

• Bind edges of quilt with strips (straight grain), cut 12 cm [4½″] wide to make double binding.

• Stitch buttons or bells in place on top of doors. Stitch loops of thread at the top of each centre square to hold doors in place.

Log cabin blocks each 20 cm [8″] square with 5 cm [2″] centre square. Strips cut 2.5 cm [1″] wide finished size.

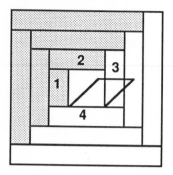

Block A

Begin sewing with strip 1, sewing it to the left of the centre square. Insert door between centre square and strip 4. For blocks 1, 7, 13, 14, 20, 23.

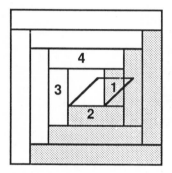

Block B

Begin sewing with strip 1, sewing it to the right of the centre square. Insert door between centre and strip 2. For blocks 2, 5, 11, 12, 18, 24.

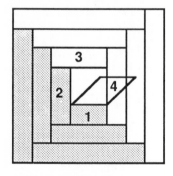

Block C

Insert door between centre square and strip 1. For blocks 3, 8, 9, 10, 19, 21.

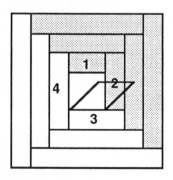

Block D

Insert door between centre square and strip 3. For blocks 4, 6, 15, 16, 17, 22.

Advent Motifs

Use linen with 28 threads per square inch. (Finished size each 5 cm [2″] square.)

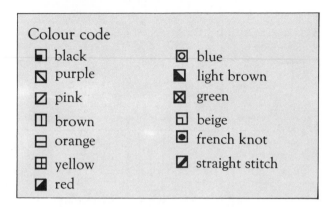

Colour code
- ◼ black
- ◩ purple
- ◪ pink
- ⊞ brown
- ⊟ orange
- ⊞ yellow
- ◥ red
- ◉ blue
- ◢ light brown
- ⊠ green
- ◲ beige
- ⦿ french knot
- ◿ straight stitch

1 Wreath   ◥ red   ⊠ green

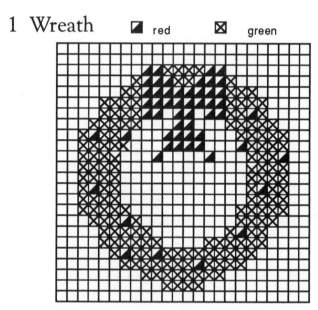

2 Christmas Tree   ◥ red   ⊠ green

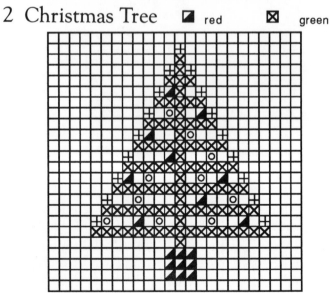

3 Decorations | straight stitch in colour to match decoration

6 Snowman

■ black ◪ red / black straight stitches
⊠ green

4 Bell ◪ red ⊠ green

7 Poinsettia ◉ red french knots

5 Drummer / black straight stitches

8 Partridge ⊞ yellow ◫ brown ◎ blue

9 Holly ◪ red   ⊠ green

12 Stocking   ◉ french knot in blue

10 Candy Cane   ⊠ green ◪ red ◿ pink

13 Presents   ┊ green straight stitch   ┃ red straight stitch

11 Plum Pudding ◪ red ⊞ brown ⊠ green

14 Santa   ◉ blue ◪ red ◿ pink ┃ black straight stitch

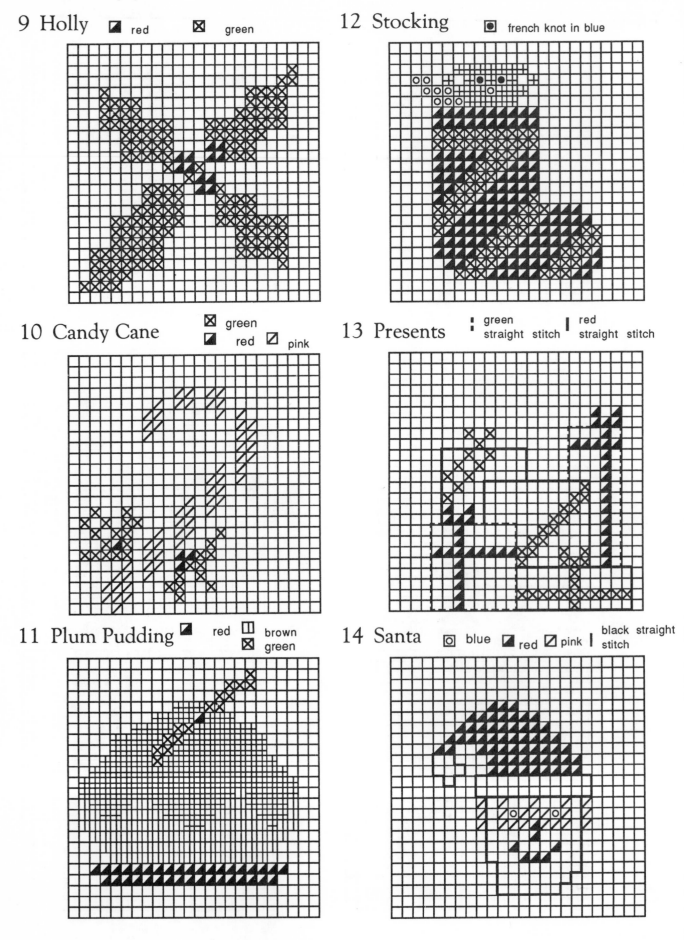

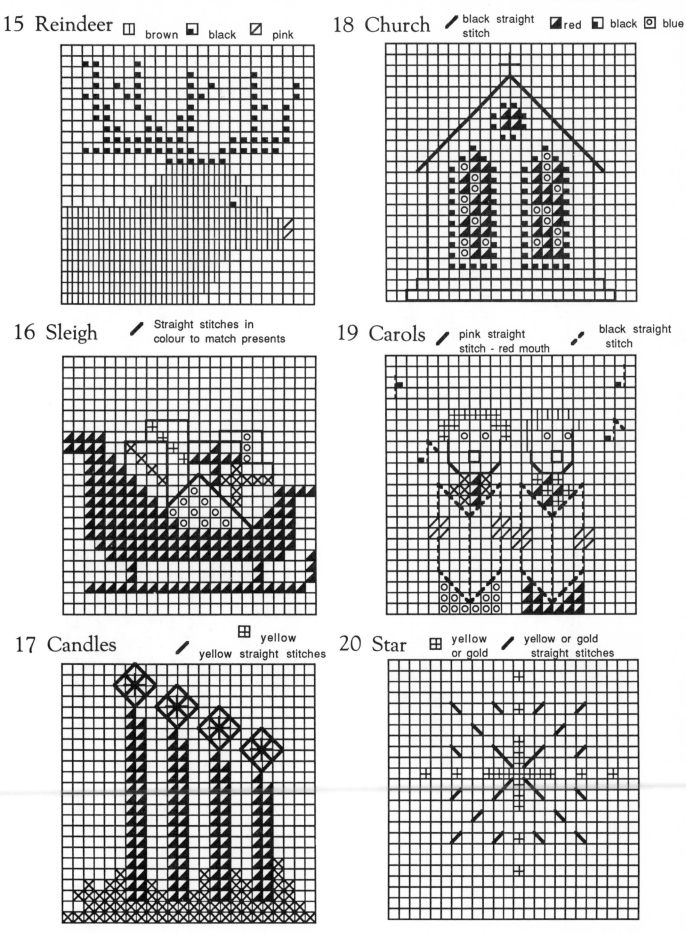

15 Reindeer ⊞ brown ◨ black ⊠ pink

18 Church ╱ black straight stitch ◩ red ◨ black ⊡ blue

16 Sleigh ╱ Straight stitches in colour to match presents

19 Carols ╱ pink straight stitch - red mouth ╱ black straight stitch

17 Candles ⊞ yellow ╱ yellow straight stitches

20 Star ⊞ yellow or gold ╱ yellow or gold straight stitches

21 Wise Men

-- : / straight stitch in colour of crown
/ straight stitch in light brown or black

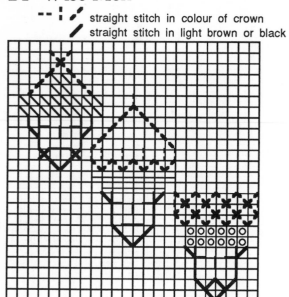

23 Shepherd

⊡ beige   ◣ light brown

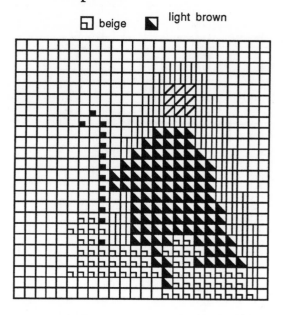

22 Angel

⊞ yellow   ⊠ pink   ⊡ blue   / blue straight stitches

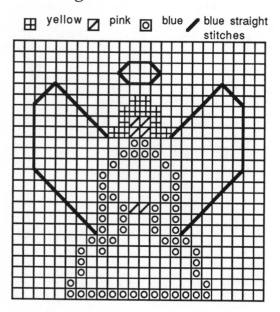

24 Nativity

-- / yellow or gold straight stitch   / brown straight stitches

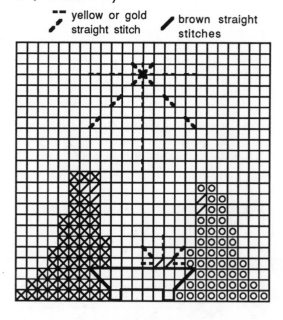

'Teddy Bear, Teddy Bear' Quilt

'Teddy Bear, Teddy Bear, turn around,
Teddy Bear, Teddy Bear, touch the ground.
Teddy Bear, Teddy Bear, show your shoe,
Teddy Bear, Teddy Bear, that will do.

Teddy Bear, Teddy Bear, go up stairs,
Teddy Bear, Teddy Bear, say your prayers.
Teddy Bear, Teddy Bear, turn out the light,
Teddy Bear, Teddy Bear, say good night.'

Finished size

102 cm square [42½"] not including binding.
Block size 24 cm [10"].

Requirements

• Background fabric for bears and outside border,
1 m [1¼ yd].

• Blue print for triangles, binding and teddy bed,
1 m [1¼ yd].

• White fabric for sashing squares and triangles,
80 cm [32"].

• Honey coloured fabric for bears, 50 cm [20"].

• Blue for bows, 10 cm [4"].

• Assortment of small pieces of fabric for applique,
including lighter honey coloured fabric for muzzle
and inner ear; black for eyes and noses; pink for
bows and bed quilt; pink and white print for bed
quilt; rust and light brown for shoes; brown for
stairs and lamp stand; lemon for lamp shade.

• Black and brown embroidery thread.

• Batting, 110 × 110 cm [48 × 48"].

• Backing fabric, 1.1 m [1¼ yd].

Template shapes for sashing

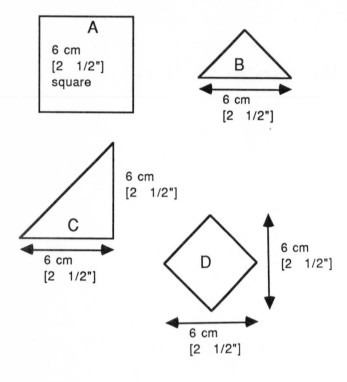

Piecing units for the sashing

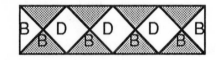

Corners   Sashing strips

Squares   Squares
in centre   at edge

Construction

• Cut out background blocks (24 cm [10″] square plus seams).

• Trace teddy bear patterns. Cut out pieces from appropriate fabrics and applique in place.

Special effects

Make pink bows out of short lengths of bias cut strips, gathering at the centre.

Make eyes and noses by cutting shapes from cardboard, gathering applique piece around cardboard and pressing well.

To make bed quilt, trace and cut out shapes of patches from paper, cover paper shapes with fabric and tack (baste) seam allowances, then overstitch shapes together from wrong side, and remove tacking.

• Embroider features on bears in black and lamp switch in brown.

• Make templates for sashing, and cut out fabric. Piece together into units as in diagram.

• Join blocks to pieced sashing as in the quilt plan.

• Add outside border.

• Assemble quilt layers. Outline quilt around bears and shapes in sashing.

• Bind edges with strips (straight grain) cut 8 cm [3″] wide for double binding.

Glossary of Quilting Terms

Applique

The process by which a piece of one fabric is stitched onto a background of another fabric. Applique is especially suited to curved and naturalistic shapes and can be sewn by hand or by machine.

Batting

The layer of padding between the top and the back of the quilt. The fibres can be made of polyester, cotton, or wool, although polyester is most commonly used today. It is sometimes called wadding.

Bias

The direction on fabric that is at a diagonal (45° angle) to the grain of the fabric (see 'Grain' below). Fabric cut on the bias has more stretch and give than fabric cut straight on the grain and this can be used to advantage when curves are required.

Block

A unit of patchwork design, and the basic unit from which most quilts are constructed. Block designs can be either pieced or appliqued.

Border

A strip of fabric (either plain fabric, a pieced pattern, or applique) which surrounds a quilt centre or quilt block, making a frame. Many quilts have multiple borders.

Grain

The direction in which the woven threads lie in a piece of fabric. Both lengthwise and crosswise threads (warp and weft) form the grain of the fabric. To match the grain means to match either of these directions. Patchwork pieces will fit together better and sit flatter if the grain is kept consistent throughout the blocks, both for piecing and applique. Templates are usually marked with a grain line to help you make the grain consistent in a block. However, sometimes you may wish to ignore the grain in order to take advantage of a special print or motif.

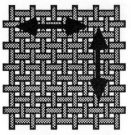 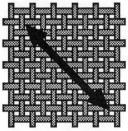

Direction of straight grain.　　　　Direction of bias.

Piecing

The process by which pieces of fabric are seamed together to make a patchwork design. The seams can be sewn by hand or by machine.

Piecing order

The term for the order in which the pieces of fabric are joined together in making a patchwork block. *Following the piecing order given is especially important for all the pictorial block designs*, because the order suggested has been carefully worked out as the easiest way to sew the block so that all the seams are straight sewing.

Sashing

The term which describes strips of fabric which surround and frame blocks in a quilt. Sashing is sometimes referred to as lattice strips.

Quilting

The process by which three layers of material are stitched together; the patchwork top, the middle layer of batting, and a layer of backing fabric. They form a textile 'sandwich'. The quilting is the stitching which joins the three layers together, and it can be done either by hand or by machine.

Strip quilting

A process in which strips of fabric are pieced and machine quilted in one operation.

Templates

The shapes, made from cardboard or plastic, which are the pattern pieces for the patchwork designs. Templates help ensure that the pieces of fabric in patchwork will be cut out accurately.

Index

Advent calendar, 132
Alphabet quilt, 59
  applique patterns, 63
  designs, 60
Applique, 150
  hand, 18
  machine, 20

Back stitch, 22
Basket quilt, 43
Batting, 4, 150
Benjamin Bunny and
    friends quilt, 98
Between needle, 2, 24
Bias, 150
Bias strips for binding,
    30
Binding, 29
Bison, 96
Blanket stitch, 22
Block, 8, 16, 150
Borders, 28, 92
Brontosaurus, 74
Buffalo, 96
Bullion stitch, 22
Bunnyrun quilt, 100
Buttonhole stitch, 22

Cardboard, 5
Cat, 58
Chain stitch, 22
Chick, 57

Circles, 20
Cow, 51
Cross stitch, 22
Cushions, 30
Cushions for sports
    fans, 39
Cutting mat, 3, 14

Daisy stitch, 22
Designs for quilting, 23
Dinosaur continental
    quilt cover, 72
Dog, 57
Dresden plate quilt, 44
Doll's quilts, 41
Duck, 55

Echo quilting, 23
Elephant, 79, 87
Elephant quilt, 78
Ele's embroidered
    quilt, 114
Embroidery stitches,
    22
Equipment, 2

Fabric, 4
  quantities, 4, 27
  transparent, 21
Farm life quilt, 47
Farmer and wife, 54,
    55

Flamingo, 88
Football stripes quilt,
    38
Free quilting, 24
French knots, 22

Giraffe, 94
Glossary of quilting
    terms, 150
Grain, 150
Graph paper, 5, 13
Grids, 10

Hand piecing, 6
Hand quilting, 23
Hen, 56
Hippo, 92
Horse, 50
House, trees and
    garden, 48

Iron, 3, 12

Ladybird bag, 111
Lion, 93
Log cabin, 17, 26, 36

Machine piecing, 8, 13
Machine quilted cot
    quilt, , 33
Machine quilting, 25

Marking and cutting
    fabric, 14
Masking tape, 3, 24
Miss Mouse quilt, 118
Mitring corners, 28
Monkey, 86

Needles, 2
Notches, 10

Ostrich, 94
Outline quilting, 23

Padding, 4
Panda, 89
Panda quilt, 102
Paper square, 3, 11
Peacock, 96
Penguin parade quilt,
    104
Pictorial blocks, 8
Pencils, 3
Piecing, 6, 151
    hand, 6
    log cabin, 17
    machine, 6
    order, 8
    regular shapes, 13
Piecing with automatic
    seam allowances, 7
Piecing with marked
    seam allowances, 7
Pig, 53
Pins, 2, 12, 21
Pinning, 12
Pinwheel quilt, 41
Planning the quilt, 27
Polar bear, 85
    baby, 108

Polar bear wall
    hanging, 106
Pressing, 12
Prewashing, 4
Protoceratops, 75
Pteranodon, 73
Puffin bag, 109

Quilt construction, 27
Quilters' quarter, 3
Quilting, 23, 151
Quilting designs, 23
Quilting hoop, 2, 24

Rhinoceros, 90
Rooster, 56
Rotary cutter, 3
    cutting shapes, 14
Rouleau, 20, 21
Running stitch, 22, 23

Sandpaper, 3
Sashing, 27, 28, 151
Satin stitch, 22
Scissors, 2
Scotty dog quilt, 82
Sea lion, 90
Seam allowances, 2, 7, 31
Set square, 3
    use with rotary
        cutter, 14
Sewing, 12, 17
Sewing machine, 2
Sheep, 52
Sheep on clover quilt,
    80
Simple squares, 32
Squares, 15

Squaring up the fabric,
    15
Stabiliser, 20
Stegosaurus, 77
Stem stitch, 22
Straight line piecing, 8
Strip quilting, 26, 151

Talking point quilt, 34
'Teddy Bear, Teddy
    Bear' quilt, 139
Teddy bear log cabin
    quilt, 36
Templates, 10, 13, 151
Thimble, 3, 24
Tied bassinet quilt, 32
Tiger, 91
Tortoise, 92
Toucan backpack, 112
Thread, 4, 6, 21, 23,
    24, 25
Tracing paper, 18
Train quilt, 45
Triangle mosaic quilt,
    42
Triangles, 16
Triceratops, 75
Tying, 23
Tyrannosaurus, 76

Varying quilt size, 27

Walrus, 97

Zebra, 95
Zoo quilt, 84